# Essential Mind Training

# ESSENTIAL MIND TRAINING

*Tibetan Wisdom for Daily Life*

Translated, edited, and introduced by

## Thupten Jinpa

WISDOM PUBLICATIONS • BOSTON

Wisdom Publications, Inc.
199 Elm Street
Somerville, MA 02144 USA
www.wisdompubs.org

Library of Congress Cataloging-in-Publication Data
Essential mind training / translated, edited, and introduced by Thupten Jinpa. — 1st ed.
    p. cm.
 Includes bibliographical references and index.
 ISBN 0-86171-263-3 (pbk. : alk. paper)
 1. Blo-sbyoṅ. I. Thupten Jinpa.
 BQ7805.E87 2011
 294.3'442—dc23

                         2011022683

ISBN 9780861712632
eBook ISBN 9780861717149

15  14  13  12  11
5   4   3   2   1

Cover design by Phil Pascuzzo. Interior design by Gopa&Ted2. Set in Diacritical Garamond Pro 10.75/12.7.

Wisdom Publications' books are printed on acid-free paper and meet the guidelines for permanence and durability set by the Council of Library Resources.

Printed in the United States of America.

This book was produced with environmental mindfulness. We have elected to print this title on 30% PCW recycled paper. As a result, we have saved the following resources: 25 trees, 10 million BTUs of energy, 2,496 lbs. of greenhouse gases, 11,258 gallons of water, and 713 lbs. of solid waste. For more information, please visit our website, www.wisdompubs.org. This paper is also FSC® certified. For more information, please visit www.fscus.org.

# Publisher's Acknowledgment

THE PUBLISHER gratefully acknowledges the generous help of the Hershey Family Foundation in sponsoring the publication of this book.

# Contents

# Preface

*ESSENTIAL MIND TRAINING* is the first publication in a new series called *Tibetan Classics*, which presents accessible softcover editions of translations of seminal Tibetan Buddhist works excerpted from the larger, hardcover volumes of *The Library of Tibetan Classics*. The original volume from which this particular anthology is drawn is *Mind Training: The Great Collection*, which I had the privilege to translate into English. Mind training, or *lojong*, is a method for transforming our habitual self-focus into a more compassionate and altruistic way of life, and it gives me great joy to be able to help present this cherished practice to a wider audience.

This selection of eighteen essential texts of the mind training tradition is accompanied by an essay in the form of an introduction, short explanations for each section of the book, explanatory endnotes, as well a glossary to assist the reader with key terms. All of these seek to provide useful context—about authorship, central themes, and historical background—to allow the reader to engage with the texts in a deeper and more meaningful way.

I would like to express my deep gratitude, first and foremost, to my two teachers, His Holiness the Dalai Lama, for being such a shining examplar of the Tibetan tradition, and Kyabjé Zemé Rinpoché, for embodying the spirit of Tibetan mind training teachings and introducing me to its wonderful world. My heartfelt thanks also go out to Barry J. Hershey, Connie

Hershey, and the Hershey Family Foundation, whose support enabled me to undertake the translation of the texts in this volume. I also want to thank Pierre and Pamela Omidyar, who, through a special grant, allowed me to develop this particular volume for a general readership.

Let me also take this opportunity to offer profound thanks to Nita Ing and the Ing Foundation and Eric Colombel and the Tsadra Foundation for their ongoing support of translating multiple volumes from *The Library of Tibetan Classics*. I would also like to thank David Kittelstrom, our longtime editor at Wisdom Publications on the classics series, whose incisive editing always makes my English look better than it actually is; Tim McNeill and his team at Wisdom Publications, for their dedication to excellence; and last but not least my wife Sophie Boyer Langri, for her unwavering support and patience in the face of my never-ending work related to classical Tibetan culture.

Thupten Jinpa
Montreal, 2011

# Introduction

WITHIN THE VAST body of Tibetan spiritual literature, one genre stands out for its inspirational power, universality, and down-to-earth practicality, qualities that have made these teachings dear to the Tibetan people for generations.[1] I am referring to a collection of texts and their associated contemplative practices known simply as *lojong*, or "mind training," which first appeared in the land of snows almost a millennium ago. At its heart the Tibetan mind training teachings represent a profound celebration of the spiritual ideal of genuine altruism, a deeply felt compassion for all beings and a dedication to serve their welfare. This is an ideal shared across many of world's great spiritual and humanistic traditions. By the twelfth century *lojong* had become a most cherished spiritual heritage on the vast Tibetan plateau, with attendant myths and legends associated with its origin and development.

Today, as interest in Tibetan spiritual teaching and insights grows worldwide, often it's the mind training teachings that are most shared with the larger world by Tibetan teachers. I vividly remember the beautiful morning of August 15, 1999, when nearly a hundred thousand people from all walks of life gathered in New York's Central Park to listen to His Holiness the Dalai Lama's exposition of *Eight Verses on Mind Training*. As on many of the Dalai Lama's trips, on that day I had the privilege to sit beside him as his official translator, and on this occasion, the beauty and simplicity of these eight short verses brought a special power and poignancy to the event. The atmosphere was pervaded by a stillness of attention, deep spiritual presence, and a shared experience of warmth toward all things living, and those present felt—at least for an hour and a half—that they had touched something deep within themselves.[2] Three years later the Dalai Lama returned once again to Central Park, and that time he chose to teach Atiśa's *Bodhisattva's Jewel Garland* to a gathering whose size exceeded even the previous meeting. Both of these seminal mind training texts are featured in the present volume.

In my own life, I have been fortunate to be exposed to the mind training teachings from an early age and have, for more than three decades now, recited the Tibetan teacher Langri Thangpa's *Eight Verses of Mind Training* on a daily basis. The story of Langri Thangpa's single-pointed contemplation of the suffering of all beings, even to the point of acquiring the nickname the "one with a tearful face," and how he came to befriend the wild animals living around his retreat imprinted in me an intuitive affinity with the Kadam lineage, which is associated with the emergence of *lojong* teaching. As a young monk, I would daydream of the idyllic scene where, as an old hermit, I would feed grass to the wild animals that would be living around my hut in some remote mountainous wilderness.

My own personal teacher at Ganden Monastery, Kyabjé Zemé Rinpoché, at whose house I had the honor to live as a monk student, was a great embodiment and master of mind training. While I was deeply immersed in the study of intricate philosophical views that was part of our regular curriculum, every now and then, Rinpoché would remind me of the critical need to be grounded in everyday reality and the need to never be disconnected from contemplating others' welfare. He would stress that, at the end of day, it's the teaching of *lojong* that helps us make the insights and wisdom of the Buddha a reality in our own lives.

On several occasions I was also able to witness at first hand the power of mind training practice to engender courage and resilience in ordinary individuals. A neighbor of mine at the monastery, an ordinary monk, suffered a debilitating skin condition that produced thick scabs on the surface of his skin, which would harden and then crack open. In the heat of the South Indian summer, he had to avoid, as far as possible, any contact between two skin surfaces, such as around the armpits and behind the knees. Though his pain and discomfort were severe, this monk, as a mind training practitioner, always maintained a tranquil and happy state of mind. This capacity to greet life's difficulties with calm and joy is one of the key indicators of success in training the mind.

In fact, there is a saying attributed to the Kadam lineage masters that the best measure of our spiritual development is how we relate to death when our final day arrives. Those most advanced in their spiritual development will face their mortality with joy; those of medium development will do so without fear. Even the least developed, we are told, should ensure that they approach their final day without any regrets.

Having spent the first three decades of my life in India, a major portion of that in the Tibetan monasteries, I was privileged to see this "measure" of spiritual development in operation. The grace and calm, the note of true freedom in their ability to let go, and the genuine lack of remorse, borne of the awareness that they have done their best while alive—these are some of the characteristic qualities of the state of mind I observed in many of the senior monks, including my own personal teacher, as they approached their own mortality. Even today, when I think of these examples of what some might call "graceful exits," the words that come easiest to mind are serenity, dignity, and grace.

## *The Meaning and Origins of Mind Training*

The Tibetan term *lojong* is composed of two syllables. *Lo* stands for "mind," "thought," or "attitudes," while *jong* connotes several interrelated but distinct meanings. First, *jong* can refer to *training* whereby one acquires a skill or masters a field of knowledge. *Jong* can also connote *habituation* or familiarization with specific ways of being and thinking. Third, *jong* can refer to the *cultivation* of specific mental qualities, such as universal compassion or the awakening mind. Finally, *jong* can connote *cleansing* or purification, as in purifying one's mind of craving, hatred, and delusion.

All these different meanings carry the salient idea of transformation, whereby a process of training, habituation, cultivation, and cleansing induces a kind of metanoesis, from the ordinary deluded state, whose modus operandi is self-centeredness, to a fundamentally changed perspective of enlightened, other-centeredness.[3] Today, thanks to research on neuroplasticity, we have a much better appreciation of the brain's capacity for transformation and change.

Broadly speaking, all the teachings of the Buddha can be characterized as "mind training" in the senses described above. However, the genre called *mind training* or *lojong* refers to specific approaches for cultivating the *awakening mind*—the altruistic aspiration to seek full awakening for the benefit of all beings—especially through the practice of equalizing and exchanging of self and others as found in Śāntideva's eighth-century classic, *A Guide to the Bodhisattva's Way of Life.*[4]

Two famous short works of the Tibetan mind training genre are today well known to the English-speaking world, with numerous commentaries by contemporary Tibetan teachers. These are Langri Thangpa's *Eight Verses on Mind Training* and Chekawa's *Seven-Point Mind Training*, both of which are contained in the present volume together with translations of their earliest commentaries.[5]

Traditional Tibetan sources identify the Indian Bengali master Atiśa (982–1054) to be the source of *lojong* in Tibet. Judging by currently available literature, the early origins of mind training as a separate genre of texts and spiritual practice appear to lie in the varied pithy instructions Atiśa may have given individually to many of his disciples. These instructions came to be later compiled under the rubric of "root lines on mind training," thus forming the basis for the emergence of subsequent *lojong* literature.

A well-known legend associated with the emergence of the *lojong* teachings is Atiśa's sea voyage to the Indonesian island of Sumatra, where he went to seek the instruction on "mind training" from Serlingpa.[6] It is from him Atiśa is said to have received the profound instruction on the techniques of "equalizing and exchanging self and others," which entails a disciplined process aimed at radically transforming our thoughts, prejudices, and habits from self-centeredness to other-centered altruism. Years later, in Tibet, whenever Atiśa uttered his teacher Serlingpa's name, it is said, he would instinctively fold his palms together in homage with tears in his eyes. "Whatever degree of kind heart I possess," he is reputed to have exclaimed, "this is due entirely to my teacher Serlingpa." Such was the depth of Atiśa's gratitude for having received the mind training instructions.

In tracing the immediate source of the *Seven-Point Mind Training*, there is a memorable passage in a thirteenth-century work that describes a brief exchange between two Kadam masters, Chekawa (1101–75), the author of the *Seven-Point*, and his

teacher Sharawa. Having been intrigued by the powerful altruistic sentiments expressed in Langri Thangpa's *Eight Verses*—
such as "May I accept upon myself the defeat / and offer to
others the victory"—Chekawa asks Sharawa whether these
teachings have a scriptural basis. The teacher then cites some
stanzas from Nāgārjuna's *Precious Garland* and asks if there is
anyone who does not accept the authority of Nāgārjuna.[7] This
story is often repeated in later literature. According to
Chekawa, several sutras and early Indian treatises stand out as
the primary sources of mind training teachings, but the most
important are undoubtedly Nāgārjuna's *Precious Garland* and
Śāntideva's *Guide to the Bodhisattva's Way of Life*.

The present book contains the seminal Tibetan works on
mind training extracted from *Mind Training: The Great Collection*, the earliest known anthology of this genre. I had the
privilege to bring a translation of the complete anthology to the
English-speaking world, and it gives me great pleasure to be
able to present here the most seminal and inspiring works from
within that collection.

## *Key Features of Mind Training*

There is no denying that, historically, the mind training teachings evolved in the context of Buddhist practitioners whose
primary goal is to seek enlightenment, in fact buddhahood, for
the benefit of all beings—the highest aspiration of a Mahayana
Buddhist. And the mind training instructions and practices
were recognized by many such aspirants to be a highly effective
set of contemplative practices to achieve this end. In addition,
it was those meditators who were single-pointedly dedicated to
the pursuit of full awakening who found these instructions to
be a source of deep inspiration and personal transformation.
One need only recall such examples as the story of the "three

Kadam brothers"—Potowa, Chengawa, and Phuchungwa; the ever-weeping Langri Thangpa; Chekawa, the teacher of the lepers; Ben Gungyal, the famed robber turned hermit; and Shawo Gangpa, who inscribed self-exhortation lines on the posts he erected in the four cardinal directions around his meditation hut.

This said, as the history of mind training testifies, much of the popularity and success of mind training teachings lie in their universality, their relevance to the everyday lives of people from all walks of life, not just serious meditators. Furthermore, since the order in which the various aspects of mind training are enacted depends principally on where we are as spiritual aspirants, as the early *lojong* teachers would say, there is something in mind training practice for everyone.

A central theme of mind training practice is the profound reorientation of our basic attitude toward both our own self and fellow sentient beings, as well as toward the events we experience. In our current naïve everyday attitude, we not only grasp at an intrinsically real "self" as being who we truly are, we also cherish this "me" at the expense of all others. We feel hurt when someone insults us, disappointed when someone we love betrays us, outraged when provoked for no reason, pangs of jealousy when others are successful, and all of these tend to strike us more intensely the stronger our self-cherishing.

The mind training teaching challenges us to question this. By deeply understanding others as friends "more precious than a wish-fulfilling jewel"—as Langri Thangpa puts it in his *Eight Verses on Mind Training*—and recognizing that our true enemy lies inside ourselves, we overturn our habitual self-centeredness. It is self-cherishing that opens us to painful and undesirable experiences. Mind training teachings admonish us to instead "Banish all blame to the single source. / Toward all beings contemplate their kindness."

This somewhat paradoxical instruction that *if we truly cherish our own happiness, we must seek the welfare of others* captures a powerful insight into our human condition. Whether in the domain of our relationships, our sense of purpose in life, or our overall degree of contentment, today researchers are increasingly telling us that what matters most is a basic feeling of connection with others and a need to care for others' well-being. In other words, modern research seems to be telling us the simple truth that excessive self-centeredness is costly, in terms of both our own personal happiness and our relationships with others and the world around us. The moral of these findings is clear: All of us, those who care for our own well-being, need to shift our basic attitude and move closer to a stance rooted in caring for others.

As an important step toward this other-centeredness, the mind training masters admonish us to view our fellow beings not with rivalry and antagonism but rather with a feeling of gratitude. We cultivate this feeling of appreciation regardless of whether others mean to be kind to us or not, for the fact is that we owe everything in our life to others. From birth to basic survival, from simple joys of eating a meal to a deeper sense of contentment, in every way, the presence of others is indispensable. Today, research on happiness increasingly points to the truth of this basic *lojong* teaching.

One of mind training's most evocative contributions to world spirituality is the practice of *tonglen*, or "giving and taking." *Tonglen* is a seemingly simple meditation practice of giving away one's own happiness and good fortune to others and taking upon oneself their suffering and misfortune. The meditation is meant to enhance loving-kindness and compassion. In mind training, this practice is combined with our breathing, whereby when we breathe in, we imagine taking from all other beings their pain and misfortune, relieving them of all their negative traits and behaviors—visualized as streams of dark clouds, as smoke, or as brackish water—entering our body. These become like an antibody, attacking the virus of excessive self-centeredness. Then, when we exhale, we imagine giving to others all our happiness and good fortune, as well as our virtuous traits and behaviors. These are visualized as white clouds, bright lights, or streams of nectar, radiating from us and entering the bodies of other beings, bringing them joy and calm. The *Seven-Point Mind Training* presents this practice most succinctly: "Train alternately in giving and taking; / place the two astride your breath."

In Tibet lamas often would advise their disciples, especially if they happened to fall ill, to focus on *tonglen* meditation. The idea is to seize the opportunity presented by your sickness to recognize the universality of suffering and creatively use misfortune to reflect on others' suffering. You might cultivate the thought, "May my suffering serve to spare others from similar experiences in the future." Imagining that you are taking upon yourself the same illness afflicting many others right at that moment, you imagine that you thereby spare them from their illness.

So *tonglen* practice helps you to be courageous in the face of suffering while at the same time empathically connecting with the suffering of others. This is a beautiful spiritual practice, which practitioners of other faiths, such as Christianity, or even of no faith, can easily incorporate into everyday life. Indeed, that is happening in many parts of the world today.[8]

Since a key goal of mind training is the radical transformation of our thoughts and habits, remedies for the various ills of the mind are a dominant feature of these teachings. To begin with, as the instruction "Purify whatever is coarsest first" puts it, there is the practical advice to tackle our most glaring mental afflictions first. Then comes the admonition to "overcome all errors through a single means," namely the cultivation of compassion.

In addition, we find the crucial injunction to ensure the purity both of our initial motivation and of our state of mind upon concluding an action. The *Seven-Point Mind Training* expresses this injunction as "There are two tasks—one at the start and one at the end."

Finally, we are advised to make our own self the primary witness to our thoughts and actions presented in the line "Of the two witnesses, uphold the primary one." A witness here means a kind of overseer, someone watching to make sure we do not go astray. If we rely only on others to be witnesses to our conduct, there will be occasions when we have no witness. And even if others are watching us, it is not always easy for them to gauge the internal states driving our actions. In contrast, we can never escape from ourselves. More importantly, if we can establish a positive self-image, then every time we encounter a situation that tempts us to behave in a way that is contrary to our self-image, we will recognize such conduct to be unbecoming and reject it. Being a witness unto ourselves in this way can be a most effective means of guarding against destructive tendencies.

If, after all of this, we fail to recognize that the ultimate nature of all things is without substantial reality, and we continue to fall prey to self-grasping, we are advised to learn to view all things from their ultimate perspective, as dreamlike. Given our deeply ingrained tendency to *reify*—to project concrete reality on to—anything we deem worthy of attention, once our remedies for self-cherishing prove successful, we risk grasping at the remedies themselves and finding ourselves still in bondage to mental afflictions. So we are told, "The remedy, too, is to be freed in its own place."

On the spiritual path we meet all kinds of circumstances,

both positive and negative. To be successful, we need a way to remain steadfast in the face of difficulties. In this, the mind training teachings excel brilliantly. The *Seven-Point Mind Training* puts it this way: "When the world and its inhabitants are filled with negativity, / transform adverse conditions into the path of enlightenment." Say we are slandered by someone with no justifiable basis; we can see the situation as a precious opportunity to cultivate forbearance. If we are attacked by someone, we can view the assailant with compassion, seeing that he is possessed by the demon of anger.

The masters of the mind training teachings extend this principle to all possible situations. They speak of taking onto the path both good luck and bad, both joy and pain, both wealth and poverty. In a beautiful stanza, the Kashmiri master Śākyaśrī, who came to Tibet at the beginning of the thirteenth century, writes:

> When happy I will dedicate my virtues to all;
> may benefit and happiness pervade all of space!
> When suffering I will take on the pains of all beings;
> may the ocean of suffering become dry![9]

When we as spiritual practitioners learn to relate to all events in this radically transformed manner, we will possess something akin to the philosopher's stone, able to transform every circumstance or event, whether positive or negative, into a condition conducive to enhancing altruism. No wonder the early mind training masters compare this teaching to an indestructible diamond, to the all-powerful sun, and to the mythological wish-granting tree. If we lived our lives according to the principles of mind training as instructed by the great masters of the tradition, we could easily relate to the sentiments of Chekawa:

> Because of multiple aspirations,
> I have defied the tragic tale of suffering
> and have taken instructions to subdue self-grasping;
> now, even if I die, I have no remorse.

One of the central themes running throughout the mind training instructions—whether it is cultivating gratitude for others' presence, or recognizing how self-destructive obsessive self-centeredness is, or transforming adversities into opportunities, or being one's own principal witness—is the notion of genuine courage. This is not a courage based in foolhardiness; rather, it is a courage rooted in a clear understanding of the complexity that is our human condition. Instead of adopting a simple stoic approach to life's inevitable sufferings, *lojong* instructions show us a different path, a way that each of us can become more connected with and caring for the complex, messy, entangled web that is the deeply interconnected world of sentient beings. The mind training teachings show us a remarkable way, whereby while maintaining courage in our immediate personal concerns, we also remain totally connected with the needs and concerns of others and learn to relate to every event from such a compassionate standpoint. This is a fine balance. The vision is this: a carefree mind rooted in a deep joy. The following stanza attributed to Atiśa captures this quality succinctly:

> He who sees as spiritual teachers
> the objects that engender afflictions—
> be they enemy or friend—
> will remain content wherever he is.[10]

For me, and perhaps for many others too, one of the greatest attractions of the mind training teachings is their earthy practicality. Unlike many other established teachings of the Tibetan Buddhist tradition, such as the rigorously systematic approach of the stages of the path teachings, the somewhat mystical approach of *mahāmudrā* and *dzokchen* teachings, or the highest yoga tantric meditations, with their ritualized deity visualizations, the mind training teachings are down to earth. In fact, the masters of mind training extol its simplicity, lack of systematic organization, and unadorned pith.

Mind training is not ostentatious, but it is nonetheless very powerful. Even a single line can be said to encapsulate the entire teaching of the Buddha, in that a single line has the power to subdue self-cherishing and the mental afflictions. Unlike other teachings, mind training has no complicated structure, no confusing outlines, and it requires no complex philosophical reasoning. From their earliest stages, the mind training teachings became a shared heritage of all the Tibetan Buddhist schools.

There is a wonderful story about how mind training teaching became public in the early stages of its development. The thirteenth-century master Sangyé Gompa speaks of how Chekawa shared the mind training instructions first with individuals suffering from leprosy. Public censure of lepers was apparently a major social issue in central Tibet at the time, and Kadam teachers were deeply concerned about this. Legend has it that even Dromtönpa himself, one of the founding fathers of the Kadam school, devoted the latter part of his life to nursing lepers and eventually became himself a victim of the disease. As word spread about the mind training teaching within the leper community, more and more lepers gathered to hear Chekawa's teaching and engage in the practice, such that the teaching came to be referred to as "teaching for the lepers."[11] Perhaps it was the mind training instructions on how to rise above both fortune and misfortune and transform adversities into opportunities for spiritual growth that provided them the much-needed solace and strength to cope with their difficult life situation.

## *Atiśa's Three Indian Masters of the Awakening Mind*

One critical element of the traditional account of the origins of the mind training teaching is the story of the "three Indian masters" from whom Atiśa is said to have received instructions on awakening mind. Chekawa's teaching, as penned by his student Sé Chilbu (1121–89), is again an important source for the legend. According to this story, Atiśa received instructions on the generation of awakening mind from three different Indian masters. The first is the teacher Dharmarakṣita, a yogi whose compassion was so great that he once cut off a piece of his own flesh and gave it to a sick man as medicine.[12] The second is Kusalī Jr., a dedicated yogi of Maitreya, who is therefore sometimes called Maitrīyogi. Finally, there is Serlingpa Dharmakīrti, whom Atiśa is said to have deliberately sought by braving a twelve-month sea voyage to the Indonesian island of Sumatra.

All biographies of Atiśa agree that, of the Indian masters on awakening mind, Atiśa held Serlingpa to be the most important.[13] From the beginning of the twelfth century, especially after the codification of Atiśa's scattered sayings by Chekawa into the well-known seven points, Master Serlingpa's instructions on the cultivation of awakening mind as transmitted to Atiśa have effectively formed the kernel of the Tibetan mind training teachings. This seven-point approach became so influential that for many later authors, especially after the fifteenth century, Chekawa's *Seven-Point Mind Training* became almost equivalent to mind training itself.

## Seven-Point Mind Training

Chekawa was one of the first teachers, if not the first, to present the key elements of Atiśa's mind training instructions in terms of seven key points. The seven points are:

1. Presentation of the preliminaries
2. Training in the two awakening minds
3. Taking adversities onto the path of enlightenment
4. Presentation of a lifetime's practice in summary
5. The measure of having trained the mind
6. The commitments of mind training
7. The precepts of mind training

That Chekawa did not actually write all the lines of the *Seven-Point* in the sense of an author composing his own original work appears fairly certain. To begin with, there are at least two versions of so-called root lines of mind training—almost all lines of which find their way into the *Seven-Point.*

One version appears as the second work in the present anthology, where it is attributed to Atiśa. It is difficult to determine with any certainty who the original author of these seminal lines was and who first compiled them into a cohesive text. However, it seems likely that these lines were based on spontaneous instructions that Atiśa gave to different individuals on numerous occasions and that were later compiled by various teachers into oral transmissions so that they would not be lost.[14] Their origin in oral transmissions is evident from their brevity and vernacular style. It is perhaps also due to this oral origin that so many redactions of the root lines came about, some of which do not demonstrate any familiarity with the others. It is on the basis of some of these different redactions that Chekawa, drawing on the instructions of his teacher Sharawa, organized the root lines according to seven points.

Following the organization of the root lines on mind training into the seven key points, the *Seven-Point Mind Training*
effectively became the root text of Atiśa's mind training teachings. This short text attracted numerous commentaries from
many great Tibetan teachers. Sé Chilbu's twelfth-century commentary compiled from Chekawa's own lectures is featured in
the present volume, and it is this text that is the source for the
root text in chapter 3. Later well-known ones include those by
Thokmé Sangpo (fourteenth century), Hortön Namkha Pal
(fifteenth century), the First Dalai Lama (fifteenth century),
and Jamyang Khyentsé Wangpo (nineteenth century). At the
beginning of the fifteenth century, thanks to Namkha Pal and
other similar commentaries on the *Seven-Point Mind Training*,
a unique transmission of the *Seven-Point* based upon the ear-
whispered instructions of the great Tsongkhapa (1357–1419)
came into being. Atiśa's mind training teachings became a particularly dominant element of pedagogy and practice in the
dominant Geluk school founded by Tsongkhapa.

Due to this diversity in the presentation of the instructions
of the *Seven-Point Mind Training*, several different redactions
of the *Seven-Point* evolved.[15] There are some variations in the
length of these different versions, with certain lines appearing
in some yet not in others. In addition, some versions present the
training in the cultivation of the ultimate awakening mind
(*bodhicitta*) in the beginning part, while others present the ultimate awakening mind toward the end.[16]

## Compilation of the Present Anthology

The original Tibetan volume from which all the texts featured
here are selected was put together by Shönu Gyalchok and his
student Könchok Gyaltsen at the beginning of the fifteenth
century. Shönu Gyalchok is said to have studied with numerous

noted fourteenth-century masters, including Tsongkhapa and Yakdé Paṇchen, but received the mind training instructions from a direct student of Thokmé Sangpo called Tsültrim Pal. As for Könchok Gyaltsen we know his dates to be 1388–1469 and that he was a known master in the Sakya tradition of the Path with Its Result (*lamdré*). As mentioned, the full text of this important anthology of mind training texts, *Mind Training: The Great Collection*, is today available in English translation under the same title. Here, however, we offer the seminal texts from within that collection for the benefit of a wider audience.

Our volume opens with Atiśa's *Bodhisattva's Jewel Garland* followed by *Root Lines of Mahayana Mind Training* and the famed *Seven-Point Mind Training*, which as explained earlier, was compiled by the Tibetan master Chekawa. *A Commentary on the "Seven-Point Mind Training"* is Sé Chilbu's synthesis of Chekawa's oral teachings. Next to follow in the volume is the pithy *Eight Verses on Mind Training* by Langri Thangpa. Langri Thangpa was reputed for the depth of his compassion for all beings; he came to be nicknamed the "Crying Langthangpa," for he was said to be constantly consumed by compassion for the suffering of all beings. The commentary on *Eight Verses on Mind Training* featured next is the earliest exposition of this root text and was composed by Chekawa. Together, the texts in chapters 1, 2, 3, and 5 constitute the fundamental source texts of the Tibetan mind training tradition.

The next three texts, as well as one commentarial work, represent the instructions that Atiśa is said to have received from his "three Indian masters of the awakening mind." The first ones, *Leveling Out All Conceptions* and its commentary, represent the instructions of Master Serlingpa of Sumatra. *Wheel of Sharp Weapons*, attributed to the Indian master Dharmarakṣita, is a piognant verse work bringing sharp awareness into our everyday lives based on a series of devastating critiques of the self-obsessed nature of our habitual thoughts and behaviors. Next, *Melodies of an Adamantine Song*, which is attributed to Maitrīyogi, presents a series of meditations on loving-kindness based on invoking Maitreya, whom the Mahayana tradition understands to be the embodiment of the loving-kindness of all enlightened beings.

Following these "Indian masters' texts," the next six works (11–16) present short instructions by Tibetan masters on particular facets of mind training. Next, the present volume features *Mind Training in a Single Session* by the famed master of Sangphu Monastery, Chim Namkha Drak (1210–85), an example of how all the key themes of mind training can be reviewed in a single session of formal sitting. The final text in the present volume is a special instruction on the meditative cultivation of universal compassion from the Indian adept Virvapa.

## Conclusion

The texts in *Essential Mind Training* present the flowering of an important spiritual culture dedicated to the perfection of the human heart by cultivating the altruistic intention. In their birthplace of Tibet, these spiritual writings have inspired, nurtured, and transformed the hearts of millions of individuals across generations. Even though the first mind training texts emerged nearly a millennium ago, the simple yet profound teachings presented in them have retained their appeal and poignancy.

There is no denying that, if put into practice, the insights of mind training can exert powerful impact in our day-to-day lives. What can be more powerful in defusing the intensity of anger toward someone than imagining that person to be as vulnerable as a defenseless child? Who can deny the power of countering jealousy or joy in another's suffering than reflecting in the following manner?

> As for suffering, I do not wish even the slightest;
> as for happiness I am never satisfied;
> in this there is no difference between others and me.
> May I be blessed to take joy in others' happiness.

This stanza from Paṇchen Losang Chögyen's famed *Guru Puja* (seventeenth century) encapsulates a key teaching of the mind training tradition, where a profound recognition of the fundamental equality of self and others with respect to the basic drive to find happiness and avoid suffering becomes the basis for generating genuine compassion for all beings.

Today, as our world becomes ever more complex, with the consequence of making even our everyday lives a source of stress and constant challenge, I believe that these practical insights of Tibetan mind training can bring great benefit to many. In my own life, during now more than two decades living in the West amid all the complexities of modern existence, I have come to appreciate more deeply the value of the Tibetan mind training teaching. Confronted with the common question of how to maintain a healthy balance between parenthood, marriage, and work, and, more specifically, having to deal with the critical challenge of how to stay sane and rooted against all the social and cultural forces pulling us in so many directions, I have found the clear and poignant wisdom of *lojong*, especially the advice on maintaining a joyful state of mind, a tremendous source of personal inspiration and strength. So by making these Tibetan mind training teachings available for a general audience, it is my sincere hope and wish that many readers will be able to share in the wonderful insights of the mind training teachings and experience their profound rewards.

# ATIŚA'S LEGACY

ALL TIBETAN SOURCES agree that the origin of *lojong*, the Tibetan mind training teaching, lies in the life and work of the Indian Bengali teacher Atiśa (982–1054), especially during his twelve-year career in Tibet that began in 1042. Atiśa's name came to be celebrated throughout the Tibetan plateau, for he is credited, to a large extent, with the revival of Buddhism in Tibet after its decline in the tenth century. Associated primarily with the famed Indian monastic university of Vikramalaśīla, Atiśa was a well-known scholar and teacher, a *paṇḍita*. Due to his fame, Atiśa came to be targeted by the rulers of the western kingdom of Ngari for invitation to teach in Tibet.

The story of the personal sacrifices, including a huge amount of gold as well the life of Lha Yeshé Ö, made by the Ngari rulers to bring Atiśa to Tibet, the skillful approaches of the Tibetan translators in cultivating Atiśa while at his Indian monastery, and how he came not only to western Tibet but central Tibet as well on the urging of his spiritual heir Dromtönpa are all well known and remain to this day a source of inspiration to many Tibetans. Atiśa's contribution to the systematic revival of Buddhism in Tibet, both in terms of study and meditative instructions, remains unmatched. From collaboration in translating major Indian Buddhist works into Tibetan to teaching the key Indian classics, from composition and exposition of his *Lamp for the Path to Enlightenment* to works on philosophy and Vajrayana, and from teaching extensively to establishing a dedicated community of monks and laity, what Atiśa accomplished in his twelve years in Tibet was truly remarkable. Over time, Atiśa came to be referred to by his Tibetan followers as Jowo Jé, "sovereign lord," as Lhachik, "the sole god," or simply as Jowo, "the lord."

The first of the two short works by Atiśa featured in our present anthology is his *Bodhisattva's Jewel Garland*. This is a short work of twenty-six stanzas, composed ostensibly as a general instructional text for spiritual aspirants. Interestingly, almost all the verses of this work are found in another text by Atiśa, an epistle he wrote to the Indian king Nayapāla, a ruler of the Pallava dynasty of his time. That epistle, entitled *Garland of Unblemished Precious Gems*, is thought to have been composed when Atiśa was in Nepal, before his arrival in western Tibet. It appears that Atiśa prepared *Bodhisattva's Jewel Garland* by drawing from his epistle to the king but tailoring it for his new Tibetan followers.

The central subject of this text is how to cultivate the way of life of a bodhisattva, both the appropriate outlook and attitude as well as the specifics of actual everyday practice. Those familiar with two seminal works of Indian Mahayana, Nāgārjuna's *Precious Garland* and Śāntideva's *Guide to the Bodhisattva's Way of Life*, will recognize clear resonances of these two important texts in Atiśa's short work. An overarching theme employed by Atiśa is the idea of seeking the "seven riches of the noble ones," as opposed to mundane riches, to fulfill our ultimate aspiration for happiness. In evoking this notion of seven riches of the noble ones, Atiśa is drawing from canonical sources attributed to the Buddha, especially those in the Vinaya, or monastic discipline, collection. The seven are faith, ethical discipline, giving, learning, regard for others, self-respect, and insight.

*Bodhisattva's Jewel Garland* does not speak of the key practice of "equalizing and exchanging of self and others" and the *tonglen* (giving and taking) practice based on that, and indeed Atiśa's *Jewel Garland* does not at first appear to have been explicitly associated with the mind training genre. Only when *Mind Training: The Great Collection* was compiled in the fifteenth century did this short work of Atiśa become part of the mind training literature. Prior to this, Atiśa's *Jewel Garland* was associated more with what came to be referred to as the "Kadam lineage of pith instructions," an esoteric set of oral teachings that was transmitted by Atiśa through to Dromtönpa, who then passed it on to Phuchungwa, one the three Kadam brothers.

In this particular set of teachings, this short work of Atiśa became the root text of an entire system of teaching and pracitce that eventually came to be enshrined in a two-volume collection known as the *Book of Kadam*.[17] On this reading, each of the stanzas of Atiśa's text came to be the basis, more specifically a springboard, to an entire series of dialogues between Master Atiśa and Dromtönpa, all of which came to be compiled as the "Jewel Garland of Dialogues." Furthermore, these stanzas also came to be used as an inspiration to delve into the narratives of Dromtönpa's past lives—analogous to the *Jātaka Tales* that present the previous lives of the Buddha—during which he is said to have engaged in the relevant practices presented in these stanzas. This second set of teachings, Dromtönpa's birth stories, came to be known as the Son Teachings of the *Book of Kadam*, while the first set of teachings is characterized as the Father Teachings.

The second of the two texts by Atiśa in our anthology is known simply as *Root Lines of Mahayana Mind Training*, which was discussed in the introduction. This is a collection of pithy sayings, each attributed to Master Atiśa, that later came to be compiled together with no particular structure. Unlike his *Bodhisattva's Jewel Garland*, this work is directly connected with the emergence of *lojong*, the Tibetan mind training teaching, and is undeniably the basis for Chekawa's famed *Seven-Point Mind Training*.

One of the beautiful things about Atiśa's two seminal texts is that, like many of world's great spiritual works, the sentiments, values, and contemplative practices presented in them have universal relevance and appeal, despite their origin in a very specific context of Mahayana Buddhism. Except for some specific elements, such as the pursuit of enlightenment as defined in a very particular way, not only can the key teachings be adopted by spiritual aspirants of different religious faiths, they can also be easily embraced and put into practice by people of no particular faith. In essence, the central message of these texts has a certain timeless quality.

# 1. Bodhisattva's Jewel Garland

*Atiśa*

Sanskrit title: *Bodhisattvamaṇevalī*
Homage to great compassion.
Homage to the teachers.
Homage to the faith divinities.

1
Discard all lingering doubts,
and strive with dedication in your practice.
Thoroughly relinquish sloth, mental dullness,
    and laziness,
and strive always with joyful perseverance.

2
With mindfulness, awareness, and heedfulness,
constantly guard the gateways of your senses.
Again and again, three times both day and night,
examine the flow of your thoughts.

3
Reveal your own shortcomings,
but do not seek out others' errors.
Conceal your own good qualities,
but proclaim those of others.

4

Forsake wealth and ministrations;
at all times relinquish gain and fame.
Have modest desires, be easily satisfied,
and reciprocate kindness.

5

Cultivate love and compassion,
and stabilize your awakening mind.
Relinquish the ten negative actions,
and always reinforce your faith.[18]

6

Destroy anger and conceit,
and be endowed with humility.
Relinquish wrong livelihood,
and be sustained by ethical livelihood.

7

Forsake material possessions,
embellish yourself with the wealth of the noble ones.
Avoid all trifling distractions,
and reside in the solitude of wilderness.

8

Abandon frivolous words;
constantly guard your speech.
When you see your teachers and preceptors,[19]
reverently generate the wish to serve.

9

Toward wise beings with Dharma eyes
and toward beginners on the path as well,

recognize them as your spiritual teachers.
[In fact] when you see any sentient being,
view that one as your parent, your child, or your grandchild.

10
Renounce negative friendships,
and rely on a spiritual friend.
Dispel hostile and unhappy mental states,
and venture forth to where happiness lies.

11
Abandon attachment to all things
and abide free of desire.
Attachment fails to bring even the higher realms;
in fact, it kills the life of true liberation.

12
When you see the factors of happiness,
there always persevere.
Whichever task you take up first,
address this task primarily.
In this way, you ensure the success of both tasks,
where otherwise you accomplish neither.

13
Since you take no pleasure in negative deeds,
when a thought of self-importance arises,
at that instant deflate your pride
and recall your teacher's instructions.

14
When discouraged thoughts arise,
uplift your mind and meditate on the emptiness of both.[20]

When objects of attraction or aversion appear,
view them as you would illusions or apparitions.

15
When you hear unpleasant words,
view them as [mere] echoes.
When injuries afflict your body,
see them as [the fruits of] past deeds.

16
Dwell utterly in solitude, beyond town limits.
Like the carcass of a wild animal,
hide yourself away [in the forest]
and live free of attachment.

17
Always remain firm in your commitment.
When a hint of procrastination and laziness arises,
at that instant enumerate your flaws
and recall the essence of [spiritual] conduct.

18
However, if you do encounter others,
speak peacefully and truthfully.
Do not grimace or frown,
but always maintain a smile.

19
In general when you see others,
be free of miserliness and delight in giving;
relinquish all thoughts of envy.

20

To help guard others' minds,
forsake all disputation
and always be endowed with forbearance.

21

Be free of flattery and fickleness in friendship,
be steadfast and reliable at all times.
Do not disparage others,
but always abide with respectful demeanor.

22

When giving advice,
maintain compassion and altruism.
Never defame the teachings.
Whatever practices you admire,
with aspiration and the ten spiritual deeds,[21]
strive diligently, dividing day and night.

23

Whatever virtues you gather though the three times,
dedicate them toward the unexcelled great awakening.
Distribute your merit to all sentient beings,
and utter the peerless aspiration prayers
of the seven limbs at all times.[22]

24

If you proceed thus, you'll swiftly perfect merit and wisdom
and eliminate the two defilements.[23]
Since your human existence will be meaningful,
you'll attain the unexcelled enlightenment.

25
The wealth of faith, the wealth of morality,
the wealth of giving, the wealth of learning,
the wealth of conscience, the wealth of shame,
and the wealth of insight—these are the seven riches.

26
These precious and excellent jewels
are the seven inexhaustible riches.
Do not speak of these to those not human.
Among others guard your speech;
when alone guard your mind.

This concludes the *Bodhisattva's Jewel Garland* composed by
the Indian abbot Dīpaṃkaraśrījñāna.

# 2. Root Lines of Mahayana Mind Training
### *Attributed to Atiśa*

Homage to the sovereign who has accomplished all
purposes and who is the glorious auspicious jewel swiftly
endowing others with great happiness.

1

First, train in the preliminaries.
For the main practice, train alternately in giving and taking.
There are three objects, three poisons, and three
    roots of virtue—
this, in brief, is the instruction for subsequent practice.

2

Commence the sequence of taking from your own self.
Place the two astride your breath.
In brief, this is the distilled essence of instruction:
In all actions, train by means of the words.

3

Relate whatever you can to meditation right now.
When both are present, take them all.
Train constantly toward the chosen objects.

4

Banish all blames to the single source.
Toward all beings contemplate their great kindness.

Train in the three difficult challenges.
There are two tasks—one at the start and one at the end.

5

Contemplate the three that are free of degeneration.
Train constantly in the three general points.
Transform your attitudes but remain as you are.
Adopt the three principal conditions.
Train in the five powers.

6

The intent of all teachings converges on a single point.
Of the two witnesses uphold the principal one.[24]
Cultivate constantly the joyful mind alone;
if this can be done even when distracted, you are trained.

    i. Do not torment with malicious banter.
   ii. Do not boast of your good deeds.
  iii. Do not be ill-tempered.
   iv. Do not be boisterous.
    v. Do not be fickle.
   vi. Do not lie in ambush.
  vii. Do not place the load of a dzo onto an ox.
 viii. Do not sprint to win a race.
   ix. Do not maintain inappropriate loyalty.
    x. Do not be sporadic.
   xi. Do not abuse this practice.
  xii. Be released through the two: investigation and
       close analysis.
 xiii. Train with decisiveness.
 xiv. Be endowed with the three inseparable factors.

7

Accomplish all yogas through a single means.
If relapsed, meditate on it as the very remedy.
Whichever of the two arises, bear them both;
Do not speak of the defects [of others].

8

Do not dwell on others' shortcomings.
Do not turn the gods into demons.
Do not seek misery as a means to happiness.
Do not depend on other conditions.
   xv. Recognize what is primary.
  xvi. Forsake all expectations of reward.
 xvii. Discard poisonous food.
xviii. Do not strike at the heart.

9

This proliferation of the five degenerations
Is transformed into the path of enlightenment.
When stability is attained, reveal the secret.

10

This distilled essence of pith instructions
Stems from the lineage of most sublime masters.
These are the root lines.

This was composed by Atiśa.

# SEVEN POINTS

*SEVEN-POINT MIND TRAINING* is perhaps the earliest work organizing the assortment of root lines on mind training attributed to Atiśa into a systematic framework of instruction and practice. Prior to the emergence of the *Seven-Point*, it appears that these root lines remained scattered, giving rise to at least several different compilations referred to as "the root lines on mind training." In addition to the one above, *Mind Training: The Great Collection* includes another distinct set of such root lines.

As a simple comparison of the *Seven-Point* to the *Root Lines on Mind Training* above reveals, the two works are closely connected. In fact, some Tibetan authors make the point that Chekawa (1101–75) should be considered more as the compiler rather than the author of the *Seven-Point*, since all the key lines of that text, if not all, are attributable to Master Atiśa himself. Even the organization of the root lines into seven points is said to come from the instruction of Chekawa's teacher Sharawa. From a very early stage, however, the famed *Seven-Point* came to be hailed as "Chekawa's *Seven-Point Mind Training*."

As noted in my general introduction, Chekawa's discovery of the mind training instruction began with his intrigue upon hearing *Eight Verses on Training the Mind*, especially the lines "May I take upon myself the defeat / and offer to others the victory." Having heard these lines, Chekawa went on to seek out the full teaching as well as its sources. This quest took him to Sharawa's monastery, where one day he saw the master circumambulating a stupa. Laying down his shawl-like upper robe on the floor, Chekawa asked Sharawa to be seated so that he could request some instructions. Thus began Chekawa's full discovery of the mind training instruction, which led to his presentation of it in seven points. After Langri Thangpa's *Eight Verses*, Chekawa's *Seven-Point* came to be the most well known and widely disseminated mind training teaching. Judging by the enormous volume of commentaries it attracted, it could be argued that the *Seven-Point* came to define what mind training is.

In terms of its literary genre, a unique characteristic of the lines of the *Seven-Point* is their pithy, aphoristic nature. Unlike *Eight Verses*, there are very few, if any, actual stanzas in the *Seven-Point*. Most of the lines are stand-alone maxims capturing an essential instruction or a specific spiritual practice. It's no wonder, therefore, that today some contemporary Western teachers of Tibetan Buddhism refer to these lines of the *Seven-Point* as "slogans." Furthermore, there is a certain orality to the lines in this text, as if they were meant to be recited aloud as you embark on the various practices presented in them. As the *Seven-Point* puts it, "In all actions, train by means of the words"; this constant use of maxims as an integral part of one's spiritual practice is an important feature of the mind training approach.

We are fortunate to have, through the commentary of Sé Chilbu (1121–89), access to the earliest exposition of Chekawa's *Seven-Point Mind Training*. That the author of this commentary studied and practiced at the feet of Master Chekawa for over two decades assures us that he knew the thoughts of his teacher quite intimately. In fact, there is no doubt in my mind that the commentary we have in our present anthology was compiled on the basis of lecture notes taken directly from Chekawa's exposition of the seven points. For example, throughout this commentary, the author frequently inserts the verb *sung* (*gsungs*), which can be translated as "said" or "taught," at the end of a sentence or paragraph. This is quite characteristic of a specific genre of Tibetan spiritual writing called *sindri* (*zin bris*), which are effectively lecture notes taken at a teaching or teachings and later compiled into a coherent text. So the verb "said" or "taught" at the end of a sentence or paragraph should be read as "the master taught" or "the master said," and "master" here refers to Chekawa.

Master Chekawa, whose personal name was Yeshé Dorjé, was born in central Tibet in the first year of the twelfth century. Although he was inspired initially to pursue a nonmonastic yogi's life and received teachings from Milarepa's disciple Rechungpa, at twenty he took ordination and became a monk. The turning point in his spiritual career came when he first heard *Eight Verses* from the Kadam master Chakshingwa and, more specifically, when at thirty years old he met Sharawa. With the founding of the monastery of Cheka, from which the epithet Chekawa is derived, he appeared to have ensured the continuation of the lineage of his teachings. On the personal level, he combined life as a hermit with his duties as the head of a monastery.

Although most renowned for his *Seven-Point Mind Training*, Chekawa is known also for another set of mind training instructions, all aimed at taking adversities onto the path of enlightenment. These instructions entail (1) taking obstacles onto the path of enlightenment through the cultivation of patience, (2) taking suffering onto the path through equalizing and exchanging self and others, (3) taking adverse conditions onto the path through turning one's adversaries into friends, (4) taking the afflictions onto the path through application of their relevant antidotes. In addition to his more practically oriented mind training works, Chekawa also composed one of the earliest works of the *druptha* genre, which contrasts the central tenets of various classical Indian philosophical systems.

# 3. Seven-Point Mind Training

## Chekawa Yeshé Dorjé

### I. Presentation of the preliminaries, the basis
First, train in the preliminaries.

### II. Training in the awakening mind, the main practice
*A. Training in ultimate awakening mind*
Train to view all phenomena as dreamlike.
Examine the nature of the unborn awareness.
The remedy, too, is freed in its own place.
Place your mind on the basis-of-all, the actual path.
In the intervals be a conjurer of illusions.

*B. Training in conventional awakening mind*
Train alternately in the two—giving and taking.
Place the two astride your breath.
There are three objects, three poisons, and three roots of
    virtue.
In all actions, train by means of the words.

### III. Taking adverse conditions onto the path of enlightenment
When the world and its inhabitants boil with negativity,
transform adverse conditions into the path of enlightenment.
Banish all blames to the single source.
Toward all beings contemplate their great kindness.

With the three views and treasury of space,
the yoga of protection is unexcelled.
By meditating on illusions as the four buddha bodies,
emptiness is protection unsurpassed.
The fourfold practice is the most excellent method.
Relate whatever you can to meditation right now.

### IV. Presentation of a lifetime's practice in summary
In brief the essence of instruction is this:
Apply yourself to the five powers.
As Mahayana's transference method is
the five powers alone, their practice is vital.

### V. Presentation of the measure of having trained the mind
The intent of all teachings converges on a single point.
Of the two witnesses uphold the principal one.
Cultivate constantly the joyful mind alone.
If this can be done even when distracted, you are trained.

### VI. Presentation of the commitments of mind training
Train constantly in the three general points.
Transform your attitudes but remain as you are.
Do not speak of the defects [of others].
Do not reflect on others' shortcomings.
Discard all expectations of reward.
Discard poisonous food.
Do not maintain inappropriate loyalty.
Do not torment with malicious banter.
Do not lie in ambush.
Do not strike at the heart.
Do not place the load of a dzo onto an ox.
Do not sprint to win a race.

Do not abuse this [practice] as a rite.
Do not turn the gods into demons.
Do not seek misery as a means to happiness.

## VII. Presentation of the precepts of mind training
Accomplish all yogas through a single means.
Overcome all errors through a single means.
There are two tasks—one at the start and one at the end.
Whichever of the two arises, be patient.
Guard the two even at the cost of your life.
Train in the three difficult challenges.
Adopt the three principal conditions.
Contemplate the three that are free of degeneration.
Be endowed with the three inseparable factors.
Train constantly toward the chosen objects.
Do not depend on other conditions.
Engage in the principal practices right now.
Do not apply misplaced understanding.
Do not be sporadic.
Train with decisiveness.
Be released through the two: investigation and close analysis.
Do not boast of your good deeds.
Do not be ill-tempered.
Do not be fickle.
Do not be boisterous.
Through this proliferation of the five degenerations
transform [every event] into the path of enlightenment.

Because of my numerous aspirations,
I have defied the tragic tale of suffering
and have taken instructions to subdue self-grasping.
Now, even if death comes, I have no regrets.

# 4. A Commentary on the "Seven-Point Mind Training"

### Sé Chilbu Chökyi Gyaltsen

Your precious body is the source of all goodness;
Amid the dark ignorance of the three worlds
you uphold the pure light that illuminates the path
  to liberation—
to you, Serlingpa, who are true to your excellent name,[25]
  I bow my head.

FOLLOWING HIS FULL enlightenment Lord Śākyamuni turned the wheel of Dharma three times, and after his entry into nirvana, the authors of the commentarial treatises elucidated these three turnings. Through the combination of the Buddha's sacred words and the commentarial treatises, the teachings flourished extensively in the world.

The doctrine is taught in terms of two vehicles, namely the Great Vehicle and the Lesser Vehicle; the Great Vehicle is divided further into two—Mantra and Perfection.[26] As far as their subject matter is concerned, all of these vehicles present, either directly or indirectly, the elimination of self-grasping and the cherishing of others—the two themes. Since there is only self-grasping to be eliminated and the well-being of others to be sought, those engaged in the practice of the Buddha's teaching must understand how to relate whatever practice they undertake to these two endeavors. You should practice in such a manner. If you are able to, your Dharma practice will then be free of error, and you will arrive at the enlightened intent of the Buddha.

"Can these two points be practiced adequately on the basis of reading the treatises?"

No. The tantras are tangled, the main treatises are disorganized, and the pith instructions remain concealed. Sealed within six parameters,[27] they require dependence on the teacher's instructions [to understand]. In particular, in the context of our present uncommon Mahayana instruction, Atiśa possessed the instructions of three teachers. First, he had what he received from his teacher Dharmarakṣita. This teacher gave away even parts of his own body by cutting flesh from his thighs. Atiśa stated that although Dharmarakṣita's philosophical views were inferior, on the basis of this practice alone, one can be certain that he had attained the great seal [of perfection]. His philosophical standpoint was that of the Vaibhāṣika tenets of the Śrāvaka school, his scriptural authority was *Garland of Three Clubs*,[28] while his analytic reasoning was based on Aśvaghoṣa's *Ornament of Sutras*[29] and the *Jātaka Tales*.

Second, Atiśa possessed the instructions received from Maitrīyogi. He was the junior Kusalī brother, and he was known as Maitrīyogi because he meditated solely on Maitreya with special focus. His philosophical standpoint was that of nonabiding [Middle Way], his scriptural authority was the sutra on the *Questions of Ākāśagarbha*, while in his analytic reasoning he followed Śāntideva's *Guide to the Bodhisattva's Way of Life* and the *Compendium of Trainings*.

Third, Atiśa also possessed the instruction he received from his teacher Serlingpa. Serlingpa's philosophical standpoint was akin to that of the non-Buddhist schools that, without relinquishing self-grasping, use it as the very ground for training. His scriptural authority was the *Teachings of Vimalakīrti*, while in his analytic reasoning he followed the *Levels of the Bodhi-sattva*.[30] This instruction stems from Ārya Maitreya. The present teaching belongs to the instructions received from teacher Serlingpa.

This, in turn, is based on the following statement from the *Teachings of Vimalakīrti*:

[Egoistic] viewing of the perishable composite is the seed of the tathāgata.[31]

Just as a lotus grows not from a level soil but from the mire, in the same way the awakening mind is not born in the hearts of disciples in whom the moisture of attachment has dried up. It grows instead in the hearts of ordinary sentient beings who possess in full all the fetters of bondage. Therefore, in dependence upon this self-grasping, it is possible to cultivate the awakening mind that exchanges self and others, which is the uncommon cause for attaining buddhahood. This very self-grasping is, therefore, the core "bone" of the buddhas.

Since the teacher Serlingpa gave this to him as the kernel of his spiritual practice, Atiśa accorded great respect and reverence to this particular teacher, more so than to his other teachers. Atiśa stated, "The little warm-heartedness that I possess is due to the kindness of my teacher Serlingpa. Because of it, my lineage has blessings." Again, Atiśa is reported to have asserted that no remedy in either the Mantra or the Perfection vehicles can be an adequate substitute for entering the gateway of this spiritual practice. Atiśa bestowed this [teaching] upon the spiritual mentor Dromtönpa as his heart remedy practice. Although Dromtönpa had many disciples, his principal students were the three brothers.[32]

Chenga Rinpoché is said to have stated that one must first equalize and then practice the exchange. "This," it is taught, "is the tradition of Maitrīyogi." Potowa is reported to have stated, "As for me, when I received it from the old layman from Radreng's forest of junipers,[33] I heard that, in the tradition of teacher Serlingpa, one must practice the exchange right from the start." Here I present the instruction of Potowa.

This has seven points:
    I. Presentation of the preliminaries, the basis
    II. Training in the two minds of awakening, the main practice
    III. Taking adverse conditions onto the path of enlightenment
    IV. Presentation of a lifetime's practice in summary
    V. Presentation of the measure of having trained the mind
    VI. Presentation of the commitments of mind training
    VII. Presentation of the precepts of mind training

## *I. Presentation of the preliminary practices, the basis*

The first point, the presentation of the preliminaries, which is the basis, is stated by the following:

**First, train in the preliminaries.**

The practitioner of this mind training must be someone who, by relying on a qualified teacher whose lineage stems from Atiśa, has trained his or her mind in the three scopes[34] in a systematic order and has thus reached a certain level. The practitioner, having generated the two awakening minds, aspiring and engaging, is cognizant of including even [the tiniest] precepts of these practices. These are the prerequisites.

To engage in the practice of the two minds of awakening, you, the practitioner, should first induce enthusiasm at the beginning of your meditation session by earnestly contemplating the following points.

Reflect on the meaningfulness of having obtained a human existence of leisure and opportunity. To prevent yourself from wasting it, think: "I must practice Dharma. And among Dharma practices, this [mind training] is the most excellent." Then reflect, "Even though I may have found a human existence of leisure and opportunity, within my life's span there is no time to spare. Since in future lives I must experience happiness and suffering as fruits of my virtuous and negative karma, this [mind training] is the most excellent virtuous activity. Even for the goal of freedom from cyclic existence, no path is more profound than this. This [training] is also the supreme cause for attaining buddhahood for the benefit of self and others." Contemplate these points not only when your enthusiasm for the training of mind is strong but also when such enthusiasm is lacking.

## II. Training in the two minds of awakening, the main practice

The second point, the training in the two minds of awakening, is the main practice. It has two parts: the ultimate mind and the conventional mind. Given the sequence in which meditative equipoise and postmeditation stages arise within a single person, these two minds are presented here in the following order. First, to train in the ultimate awakening mind, there are two parts: the actual meditation session and the subsequent period practices.

### A. Training in ultimate awakening mind
### 1. The actual meditation session

The meditation session is threefold—preparatory practices, the main practice, and the concluding practice. As for preparation, undertake the seven-limb practice in your sacred space,[35] make supplications to meditation deities and your teachers, and having seated yourself comfortably on your meditation cushion, count your breath—exhalation and inhalation—twenty-one times. With these practices, you make your body, speech, and mind fit for meditative concentration. Then generate, as a precursor, the conventional awakening mind accompanied by the beneficial qualities of meditative concentration.

During the main session, given that all of these [mind training practices] depend on the tradition of "simultaneous engagement," you should simultaneously meditate on the emptiness of all phenomena, including your own self and others. Although this is true, during the preparatory stage you must relate to these phenomena in a gradual manner, enumerating each phenomenon by means of the wisdom of discriminative awareness. This, the master said,[36] has the benefit of allowing the moisture of tranquil abiding to give birth to the shoots of realization.

Next, the initial meditation on the absence of intrinsic existence of perceived objects is presented in the following line:

**Train to view all phenomena as dreamlike.**

This entire world of the external environment and the beings within it, which are by nature mere appearances, are nothing but apparitions of your own deluded mind. Thus not even a single atom exists with a reality separate from the mind. When you examine thus, you will come to realize that, even on the conventional level, no referent of your cognition is established as possessing substantially true existence. Contemplate in this manner.

Next, the meditation on the absence of the intrinsic existence of perceiving subjects is presented in the following line:

**Examine the nature of the unborn awareness.**

Contemplate thus: Similar [to the preceding meditation], the very mind that negated the intrinsic existence of the perceived objects [1] in terms of its past is no more, [2] in terms of its future is yet to be, and [3] in terms of its present is composed of three parts. It is devoid of color, shape, and spatial location; it cannot be said to be located in any specific point of the body; when analyzed, it is empty of all identifiable characteristics. [The perceiving mind too] abides as primordially unborn.

Next, the meditation on the absence of the intrinsic existence of phenomena is presented by the line:

**The remedy, too, is freed in its own place.**

Thus, the very mind that applies the remedies through seeing the emptiness of all phenomena, including your body and mind, is not established. In general, all objects of knowledge can be said to be either objects or minds. Furthermore, since we have already examined the mind, in its general form, to be devoid of intrinsic existence, you should think, "Certainly nothing is established primordially as substantially real." Free the mind of conceptualization in this manner and release it in this state of nongrasping at intrinsic nature in terms of any of the three times. Focus the mind with ease, lucidity, and vibrancy, not allowing it to fall under the influence of either dullness or excitation. This is presented by the next line:

**Place your mind on the basis-of-all, the actual path.**[37]

Identify the ordinary mind and place it in a state free of negation or affirmation. Since all seven consciousnesses are conceptual, relinquish them. The essential point is to avoid being tainted by the conception of subject-object duality. Subsequently, whenever concepts arise, by observing awareness with awareness, let them rest free within reality itself. Since this constitutes actual clear-light meditation, keep your sessions intense but brief; within one session, you can have many subsessions. As for the length of the meditation session, it is said that "the best session should have a stable base and end in a state of joy." At the conclusion, upon dissolving your visualizations, cultivate great compassion for those without such realization. Thinking, "I will place all beings in the undistorted truth of such ultimate mode of being," dedicate all your virtues for the benefit of others. Then slowly uncross your legs and perform the seven-limb rite[38] inside the sacred space.

## 2. The subsequent period [practices]

How to train in the subsequent practices is presented by the following:

### In the intervals be a conjurer of illusions.

The subsequent periods must be cultivated without losing the flavor of your meditative equipoise. Therefore, even though perceptions of self and others, the external environment and the beings within it, and so on arise, it is your delusion that causes nonexisting things to appear [as existing]. Contemplating such things as indistinguishable from illusory horses and elephants, relinquish clinging to substantial reality. Although you perceive yourself in terms of your five aggregates, you are but an appearance of the mere aggregation of dependently originated things. Apart from this, no self possesses a permanent and unitary nature. Contemplate and see yourself as an illusory person who comes and goes and interacts with objects.

Do not remain blank, thinking nothing; instead be sustained by mindfulness, and the instant something appears to the senses, think, "This too is like an illusion; it is dreamlike." In this way, you should engage with objects on the basis of such adages.

As you view all things in this manner, during the subsequent periods your mind does not become remote from the dreamlike experience of the meditation session. In this way, in the intervals between sessions, turn all your virtuous activities into the path. Abide thus in the great union, retaining the experience of the meditation session throughout all activities. To drive home these points, the master declared the following stanza and explained the practices of the relevant points together with their benefits:

> Thus ensure that all your practices remain
> untainted by the clinging of grasping at real entities
> and spread them across the vast spacelike great emptiness;
> you will then travel in the sphere of immortal great bliss.

## B. Training in conventional awakening mind

Second, the conventional awakening mind of exchanging self and others is presented. This has been taught by Śāntideva. For example, he states:

> He who wishes to quickly rescue
> both himself and others
> should practice the secret instruction:
> the exchange of self and others.[39]

> If you do not thoroughly exchange
> your own happiness with others' suffering,

you will not become a buddha.
Even in samsara you'll have no joy.[40]

From now on, to lessen harm to yourself
and pacify the sufferings of others,
give your self to others
and protect others as you would your self.[41]

This, in turn, has two parts: the actual meditation session and
the subsequent periods.

## 1. The meditation session

The way to practice during the meditation session is presented
by the following:

**Train alternately in the two—giving and taking.**

Seated on a comfortable cushion, visualize your dear mother
vividly before you. First, to cultivate loving-kindness and compassion, reflect as follows:

"Because my mother first gave me this human existence of
leisure and opportunity, which she nurtured without negligence, I have encountered the Buddha's teachings. Because of
this it is now possible to grab happiness by its very snout.[42]
She has thus helped me. Throughout all stages of life, when I
was in her womb and after birth, she nurtured me with
impossible acts of kindness. Not only that, since samsara's
beginningless time, she has constantly looked upon me with
eyes of love, perpetually held me with affection, and repeatedly protected me from harm and misfortune. She has given
me so much benefit and happiness and has thus embodied
true kindness."

Reflect thus and cultivate a depth of emotion such that tears fall from your eyes and the hairs of your skin stand on end.

Reflect: "How sad that she, my kind mother, has been wandering in the infinite cycle of existence with so many kinds of sufferings, all the while working for my benefit. In return, I will now help her by providing her benefits and happiness. I will protect her from harm and all misfortune." You should reflect in this manner.

What harms this dear mother? Suffering harms her directly, while the origin of suffering injures her indirectly. So while thinking, "I will take all these upon myself," take into your own heart in clean swaths—as if layers sheared off by a sharp knife—all the sufferings, their origin, the afflictions, and the subtle obscurations to knowledge along with their propensities, all of which exist in your dear mother. This is the meditation on the "taking" aspect of awakening mind.

Again, thinking, "I myself will seek the complete happiness of my dear mother," unconditionally offer your body, wealth, and all your virtues to your mother. This is the meaning of the following lines of *A Guide to the Bodhisattva's Way of Life*:

> To accomplish the welfare of sentient beings,
> I will make my body into a wish-fulfilling jewel.[43]

Imagine therefore your body, wealth, and roots of virtue as precious wish-fulfilling jewels. From these emerge for your dear mother all the conditions for engaging in spiritual practice, such as food, clothing, shelter, helpers, as well as devotion to a spiritual teacher—all the conditions favorable to the attainment of enlightenment—whatever she wishes. Imagine, because of this, that your dear mother completes the accumulations and attains buddhahood. This is the meditation on the "giving" aspect of awakening mind.

In this manner, first cultivating loving-kindness and compassion, combine giving and taking; undertake their practices
so that your heart becomes even more moist and ripe than
before. As you train in this manner and become capable of making an actual exchange—that is, allaying your dear mother's sufferings and seeking her happiness without counting the cost to
yourself—you have reached a degree of success in this practice.
The measure is that were your mother reborn in the hells, you
would plunge without hesitation into the burning flames to res-
cue her.

Then proceed to the second session. First cultivate love and
compassion toward all sentient beings; then reflect: "When I
generated the mind of awakening, I gave my wealth and roots
of virtue to all sentient beings; I pledged to accomplish their
welfare, taking this responsibility upon myself. I must now
actually undertake this." As before, combine giving and taking
and train in them. Here, when you engage in giving, imagine
that each and every sentient being receives a complete set of
your body, wealth, and virtues. Give these away wholeheart-
edly and with no conceptual elaborations. Thinking, "Whosoever desires, take them; do with them whatever you wish,"
regard yourself as a medicinal tree. Discarding joy and sadness,
train with the mind and recite the words aloud.

Pray, "May my body, wealth, and roots of virtue that I have
given away unconditionally become food, drink, and clothing
for those who lack them; may they become shelter for those
who lack shelter." In this way, think, "May I become the sole
cause of the happiness of both samsara and nirvana for all sentient beings; may I become the cause for eliminating all their
sufferings; may all higher qualities and fruits of the path of all
sentient beings come into being in dependence upon me." Train
with your mind and recite these prayers as well.

When training in this way, rejoice by thinking: "As the buddhas have no aim besides the welfare of sentient beings, joyous indeed it is that I have the opportunity to enact from this very instant the heart practice of the great lord of the ten levels."[44] Again, take upon yourself the subtle obscurations to knowledge that exist within the śrāvakas, the pratyekabuddhas, and the noble bodhisattvas abiding on the levels, and as you give them your three factors [body, wealth, and roots of virtue], imagine that, as a result, they complete their accumulations and attain buddhahood. These noble beings can be either included in the general category of beings or visualized separately. Choose whichever is most convenient.

**Place the two astride your breath.**

Train in the two, giving and taking, in relation to your in- and out-breaths. This makes it easier to sustain your mental focus, because the breath is readily available, and this method combats many false modes of conceptualization.

## 2. The subsequent period

The subsequent period [practices] are presented in the next line:

**There are three objects, three poisons, and three roots of virtue.**

In subsequent periods, train your mind by purifying the fields of your experience. When you experience emotions like attachment, anger, and delusion in relation to sights, sounds, and so on that are attractive, unattractive, or neutral, train the mind as follows: "Sadly, just as I indulge my sensual cravings now, countless beings in the universe are overwhelmed by desire, indulging in countless negative acts." Extract all of these [desires of other beings] in a single gesture, taking them into your heart and praying, "May all these sentient beings be endowed with the virtuous root of nonattachment." In the same way, extend this practice to all five poisons.[45]

**In all actions, train by means of the words.**

This line refers to training the mind even by means of mere words. You can do this, for instance, by reciting the following lines from a treatise:

> May the sufferings of all beings ripen upon me.
> Through my virtues, may they all achieve happiness.[46]

Alternately, you can recite the following when no one is around: "May all sentient beings' sufferings and their causes ripen upon me, and may my own self be subdued and made no more. May my virtues ripen on all sentient beings, and may they become endowed with happiness." From your very bones, cultivate the thought "O my dear mother, my dear brother and sister sentient beings! Most dear indeed are all these beings!"

This training by means of words in your four everyday activities[47] involves following the sutra's admonition to cultivate loving-kindness by means of mere words.

*III. Taking adverse conditions onto the path of enlightenment*

The third, taking adverse conditions onto the path of enlightenment, is presented by the following:

**When the world and its inhabitants boil with negativity, transform adverse conditions into the path of enlightenment.**

Whatever misfortunes befall you, whether caused by living beings or by the elements, are fruits of your own past negative actions. Misfortunes are viewed as adversities and obstacles by those unfamiliar with Dharma. But for someone who has entered the gateway of Dharma, the master said, they are exactly like what Chengawa explained to Shawo Gangpa: "If someone has mind training, all of this—physical illness and mental suffering—becomes a skillful means through which you receive the blessings and higher attainments of the teachers and the Three Jewels." Therefore, transform every circumstance into a factor that instills in you the awakening mind.

This has two parts: (A) training in the two awakening minds (the extraordinary thoughts) and (B) striving in the dual practice of accumulation and purification (the extraordinary activities).

## A. Training in the two awakening minds, the extraordinary thoughts
### 1. Taking adverse conditions onto the path of enlightenment by means of training in the conventional awakening mind

Taking adverse conditions onto the path by means of the conventional awakening mind is taught first. So how do you take these onto the path?

Reflect: "Since beginningless time I have failed to distinguish properly between enemies and friends; I have failed to recognize what is to be relinquished and what is to be adopted. I have erred, for whatever spiritual practices I have pursued have all been expressions of self-grasping. I have become no more intimate with liberation and [the Buddha's] omniscience. Today, therefore, I will properly distinguish enemies from friends and ensure the success of my Dharma practice. From now on, my own self is the enemy, and sentient beings are the friends. Beyond viewing my self as my enemy and relinquishing myself and viewing others as friends and cherishing them, nothing else is to be done."

## a. Recognizing your own self as the enemy

The reason why your own self is the enemy is presented by the next line:

**Banish all blames to the single source.**

This line presents seeing your self as the enemy. Whatever befalls you, without blaming others, think, "This is due to my own self-grasping." In this way, cast out all the resentments you hold inside. It has been taught:

> Whatever harms are in the world,
> whatever dangers and sufferings are in the world—
> all of these arise from grasping at self;
> what good is this great demon for me?

Also:

> If there is "self," recognition of "others" arises;
> on this division into self and others, grasping and
>     anger arise;
> and in relation to these two emotions,
> all calamities come into being.[48]

Also:

> Recognizing myself as flawed
> and others as an ocean of higher qualities,
> I will thoroughly discard grasping at self
> and practice embracing others.[49]

Reflect, "All my shortcomings and defects come from grasping at selfhood. From beginningless time, I have held on to a self when there was none. Wherever I was born, though there was no self, I have grasped my body as [the basis of my] selfhood. Taking its side, I have resorted to rejection and affirmation depending on whether I deemed something desirable or undesirable. In this way I have committed all three—deception, duplicity, and deviousness—toward others and, as a consequence, have accumulated afflictions and negative karma again and again. This has compelled me, since beginningless time, to endure the incalculable sufferings of cyclic existence in general and the unfathomable sufferings of the three lower realms in particular. Still, as stated in the following:

> Although countless eons have passed
> with such great hardships,
> you have sought only suffering.[50]

"As long as I fail to view this self as the enemy, I will continue to seek its well-being. As a result, I will accumulate negative karma compelling me to wander further in this infinite cycle of existence, where I will suffer more and longer than before. So this cherishing of self brings all the sufferings of the three times. Since this self has been my executioner and enemy from beginningless time, then in my every death in the beginningless cycle of existence, no one else has done the killing. Rather I have slain myself!" As if biting your lower lip,[51] firmly hold your own self as the enemy.

Where is this enemy? It is in your own heart. Śāntideva illustrates this, for example:

> If this ancient enemy long settled,
> the sole cause of steadily increasing hosts of harms,

has found its home within my very heart,
how can there be joy for me within this cyclic exisence?[52]

Think that this kind of behavior—living on the head yet denying victory to the eyes—is most inappropriate.[53] Thus the focus
or the site of this self-grasping, which is the source of all defects,
is the very body you are born into. Since beginningless lifetimes
you have held on to an "I" when there was none and have held
on to a self when there was none. Self-grasping is fraught with
defects and is the source of all sufferings. So to cherish, look at,
and protect this discolored human corpse—a lump of pus and
blood and a sack of mucus—is like carrying a bag of thorns on
your back while naked! Happiness would result if you let go,
but instead you believe that pursuing self-interest will bring
happiness, and you thus sink ever deeper into suffering as
though you craved it. Śāntideva, too, states:

> Whatever suffering is in the world
> comes from seeking your own happiness,
> while whatever happiness is in the world
> comes from the wish for the happiness of others.

> What need is there to say more?
> The childish pursue their own interests,
> while the buddhas act for the welfare of others:
> observe the difference between the two.[54]

Among all the afflictions that have harmed you since beginningless time, this self-grasping is the worst. This jealous, evil-
ridden force that causes beings to commit negative acts against
all other beings, from high spiritual teachers to lice, resides
right here within. It blocks the attainment of freedom from
cyclic existence and ties beings further into bondage. This force

welcomes all human and nonhuman agents of harm. This owl-headed betrayer[55] is the very mind that grasps on to "I" or "self" and seeks only its own selfish ends. Thinking in this manner, recognize the enemy as the enemy. Śāntideva states:

> In all the hundreds of world systems
> of cyclic existence, this has harmed me.
> Rouse your vengeance thus
> and destroy thoughts of self-interest.[56]

If you still feel unable to eradicate this self-grasping, then cultivate the following thought: "This time it is different. Today I have sought a spiritual teacher, I have read the sutras, and as a result I have now recognized the enemy!" It has been stated:

> The old days when you could
> ruin me at will are now gone;
> I can see you now, so where are you off to?
> I will tear down your arrogance.[57]

Reflect along these lines, and whenever any self-centered thought arises, the master said, be vigilant and strike the snout of this boar with a cane. This is why it is said that all the teachings of the Great Vehicle contain only the two themes: (1) totally letting go of self-grasping and (2) upholding sentient beings with deep concern and, on this basis, crippling this self-grasping and nurturing sentient beings as much you can.

Furthermore, since all the sacred scriptures and treatises were taught to subdue the afflictions, it is the afflictions they must subdue. In general there are 84,000 afflictions, which can be subsumed into 212 classes.[58] They can be further subsumed into the six root and twenty derivative afflictions. These, too, can be further subsumed into the five or three poisons, and

when subsumed further still, they are reduced to a single affliction, namely self-grasping alone. Whosoever has subdued it to
the highest degree enjoys the highest degree of happiness; to a
medium degree, a medium degree of happiness; and to a minimal degree, a minimal degree of happiness. He who has not
subdued it at all will enjoy no happiness at all. So the root of
suffering is self-grasping; and since all faults and defects are
contingent upon it, you must abandon from now on any clinging to your body and mind and regard these instead as your enemies. Most importantly you must abandon your clinging to the
body. On this point Śāntideva states:

> If I am attached to my body,
> fear arises from even slight dangers.
> This body that brings so much fear—
> who would not detest it like an enemy?[59]

Reflect, "Although I have striven hard since beginningless time
to benefit this body, it is in the nature of a material object and
thus feels no joy or pain in relation to any benefit or harm. As
for the mind, it is devoid of substantial reality and empty. Since
what appears conventionally right now comes into being from
causes and conditions, it is devoid of intrinsic identity. Furthermore, since the causes and effects cease every moment, nothing
is established following its origination. Therefore think, "Until
now I have been preoccupied with worthless, ruinous pursuits.
Starting now I will regard my own self as the enemy and call
upon all eight classes of worldly gods, demigods, and demons,
and all eighty thousand families of obstructive forces to with-
draw their defense of this self." Train with the thought "Be my
ally and help vanquish this self-grasping; help make my five
aggregates appear devoid of substantial reality and empty."

By engaging in these practices to the best of your ability, the master entreated, strive to subdue this self-grasping demon during your brief life.

Shawo Gangpa states: "If we fail to see our own self as the enemy, no one, not even our teachers, can save us. If we see it as the enemy, benefits will ensue."[60]

So if you view your own self as the enemy, even when harms brought on by hosts of nonhumans and malevolent elemental spirits befall you, these become harms perpetrated against the enemy. They become allies in your battle against self-grasping. Since they are a powerful army on your side, it is inappropriate to generate anger toward these agents of harm; look on them instead with joy. At some point in your future, the master said, a true spiritual practice will emerge that can free you from the narrow ravines of adverse conditions. At that point you should train in [the recognition of others as] friends. In this way, train now to view self and others, respectively, as enemy and friends.

Occasionally, you should train your mind also by drawing a distinction between enemy and friend even within yourself. You can give your lay name to your thoughts and actions concerned with the pursuit of your own welfare and your ordination name to your thoughts and actions concerned with the pursuit of others' welfare. Then, following the example of the spiritual mentor Ben, correlate your arms, right and left, to avoidance of nonvirtue and adoption of virtuous acts. The spiritual mentor Ben states: "My only task is to stand guard with a short spear of antidote at the entrance of my mind. When the afflictions are vigilant, I too am vigilant; when they are relaxed, I too am relaxed."[61] Also, "Be vigilant and strike the snout of each boar with a cane and chase it." All the sutras and commentarial treatises demonstrate that there is no other task besides eliminating self-grasping.

These, then, present the perception of one's own self as the enemy and the elimination of self-grasping. It is because of Sha-wopa's teachings we have the expression "the practice for smashing the demon's head."

## b. Recognizing sentient beings as friends and cherishing them

Second, viewing sentient beings as friends and cherishing them is presented by the line:

**Toward all beings contemplate their great kindness.**

Shawopa calls this "the spiritual practice of carrying the flesh and carrying the blood." It is called "the practice of accepting all ill omens as charms." Here you deliberately focus on the perpetrators of harm and cultivate loving-kindness and compassion and then train in giving and taking.

First is the meditation on loving-kindness. Reflect, "These humans and nonhumans, who inflict harm upon me, have been related to me so many times as my parents, siblings, and friends—the frequency of which is greater than the number of *kolāsita* nuts [required to cover the face of the earth].[62] They have constantly looked at me with eyes of love, perpetually sustained me with affectionate hearts, and constantly guarded me from harm and unhelpful situations. They have granted me all kinds of advantages and happiness and are thus embodiments of true kindness." Reflecting thus, develop deep and earnest empathy for them; feel as though, were you able to place them deep within your heart, you would still not be content. View them as pieces of your own heart. Atiśa refers to beings as "my divinities" and "my spiritual teachers."

The meditation on compassion is as follows. Reflect, "They harm me today not willfully but out of a deluded mind. I have pursued my own self-interest since beginningless time, without regard to negative karma, suffering, or disrepute, and I have thus accumulated afflictions and negative karma. Because of this I have wandered in this infinite cycle of existence, embracing misery as practice. The blame for all of this lies in the self. Even at present, in my quest for enlightenment for the benefit of self and others, as I uncontrollably exploit and create obstacles for my dear mothers because of my negative karma, I am causing obstacles to the happiness of all sentient beings. So the blame for their departing to the hells in their future lives lies also in me. This is most sad indeed!" Cultivate compassion as intense as a hot coal on your bare flesh. In this manner, cultivate loving-kindness and compassion focused specially on the perpetrators of harm.

If you cultivate loving-kindness and compassion in this manner, because nonhumans have some karmically acquired clairvoyance, the moment you recognize them as your mothers, they will recognize you as their child. When this mother-child attitude emerges, how can they inflict harm? It is a law of nature that when I relate to someone as my mother, she will in turn relate to me as her child. This alone can alleviate your suffering. The *Condensed Perfection of Wisdom* states:

> The world of humans is replete with elemental spirits
> and diseases,
> but these are pacified with power of truth by those
> who care and have compassion.[63]

When you cultivate loving-kindness and compassion toward the perpetrators of harm, you arrive at the following realization: "Since beginningless time, they have only benefited me, yet I have given only harm in return. Therefore, from now on, I shall help them and protect them from harm." With this thought, combine the two practices of giving and taking and train your mind. Take upon yourself all leprosy and sickness in the world.[64] Heap upon your present sickness all the negative karma within your own life, all that you are likely to reap in the remainder of your life or in your future life, and rejoice.

Again, train as follows. Invite the malevolent nonhuman spirits to the space before you and declare: "The number of times you have been my mother is beyond count. Also, if I were to pile together the number of times I ate your flesh, drank your blood, chewed your bones, wore your skin, and sucked your milk, even the entire trichilicosmic universe would be too small to contain it all. I have also killed you, assaulted you, and robbed you countless times. Today you have merely come to collect the debt. Today please take as payment all these kind acts and offerings. It is appropriate that you own me, for you have been most kind indeed."

Reflecting thus, declare: "Devour my flesh if you like flesh! Drink my blood if you like blood! Chew my bones if you like bones! Peel away my skin and wear it if you like skin! Eat me raw if you are in haste, and if not, then eat me cooked!" Potowa is reported to have expressed:

> I offer ritual cakes in the four directions
> to all beings of the six realms
> How much I yearn for the time
> when I'm devoured and carried away by insects!

Then imagine that the nonhuman spirit rises up instantly and devours you from head to heels, smearing his mouth with your blood. His body now full, his harmful intentions disappear, and he becomes endowed with altruistic thoughts. Imagine that, as a byproduct, your negative karma becomes cleansed. Imagine that a moment later, your body rematerializes and is again devoured. Visualize this over and over. Imagine that your body is cut into a hundred or a thousand pieces, and these are then offered everywhere. In particular, share this body and mind in places of special sensitivity [such as cemeteries]. Then, with the thought "This body of mine belongs to him," undertake all virtuous practices for [the nonhuman spirit's] sake. Even the concluding dedication should be done on his behalf. In particular, where such nonhuman forces reside, mentally discard your body, and cutting it open right there, with blood soaking everything, offer it with the thought "Now eat!" Then let go of cherishing your body as stated:

> I have already given this body
> to all beings to do with as they please.
> Let them do with it whatever they wish, such as
>     beating it;
> why should I be concerned?[65]

These lines present the practice of regarding sentient beings as friends and cherishing them. Thus it is necessary to train your mind by distinguishing between the two classes—enemy and friend.

Shawopa states: "Search for the enemy in oneself; search for a god in the demons; search for virtues in nonvirtues; and search for happiness in suffering."

Langri Thangpa, too, says: "No matter what profound scriptures I open, I find none that do not suggest that all faults are your own, and that all higher qualities belong to brother and sister sentient beings. Because of this, you must offer all gain and victory to others and accept all loss and defeat for yourself. I have found no other meaning."

Shawopa states: "If someone finds a meaning other than this, it is an error." In brief, the master said, no other intent can be found in all the scriptural collections. With this, the taking of adverse conditions onto the path of enlightenment by means of conventional awakening mind has now been presented.

## 2. *Taking adverse conditions onto the path by means of training in ultimate awakening mind*

Following this, the second, taking adverse conditions on to the path of enlightenment by means of training in ultimate awakening mind, is presented in the following:

> **With the three views and treasury of space,**
> **the yoga of protection is unexcelled.**
> **By meditating on illusions as the four buddha bodies,**
> **emptiness is protection unsurpassed.**[66]

Conclude decisively that everything in this world of appearance, both the external environment and the beings within— for example, the victim and the perpetrator—are only deluded perceptions of your own mind. As mere deceptive, deluded appearances, both sides will cease within moments, with no time either to injure or to engage in any negation or affirmation. Even conventionally, nothing exists as an object or agent of harm. On the ultimate level no phenomenon is primordially established. Like the center of a spotless sky, phenomena are all one.

Since self is an instance of awareness that is devoid of substantial reality, and the agent of harm is an instance of awareness devoid of substantial reality as well, neither exists as the victim or the perpetrator. Everything is empty, and emptiness cannot be attacked by emptiness. Just as the eastern part of the sky cannot cause harm to the western part, they [the harmed and the harmer] cannot injure each other. Therefore, since your current perceptions are illusions of a deluded mind—the self, the victim, and the ailments—other than being constructs of your mind, they do not exist with any sort of identity. It is taught:

> Your own mind is Māra;
> your own mind is the obstruction;
> all obstructions arise from conceptualization;
> therefore relinquish conceptualization.[67]

Because you have grasped your concepts as real, as true, as something separate from the mind, and as fault-ridden, this has produced all the sufferings of cyclic existence. Apart from your own conceptualization, nothing outside is an obstructor; therefore your own conceptualization is the sole thing to be eliminated. When examined in this manner, everything comes down to your mind; and the mind, too, when examined, is found to be emptiness. There is no difference between the clear-light nature of your own mind, the clear-light nature of the minds of all sentient beings, and the pristine cognition of the Buddha's enlightened mind; they are equally dharmakāya—the buddha body of reality. So who can be harmed? Who causes the harm? And how is anyone harmed? Ultimately, nothing exists as a separate reality. Conventionally, however, all illnesses and malevolent forces exist as your own concepts. Reflecting that "The concepts [too] exist as dharmakāya," place the mind naturally at rest, free of any conceptualization. Like throwing up vomit, place your mind free of all clinging. Like the corpse of a leper, discard it as if it were of no use. Like a dead person's [abandoned] empty house, let it be without clinging.

Reflect: "Phenomena are not established primordially, yet I remain bound, as though unable to undo knots made in the sky or strangled by a tortoise-hair noose.[68] As such, my mind has arisen as a demon, and chained by conceptualization, I remain enmeshed in suffering." All hopes and fears, such as fearing illness or harm from ghosts, or hoping to be cured of illnesses, as well as all thoughts of negation and affirmation in emptiness: place them all within the sphere of emptiness and release them within ultimate reality itself.

Imagine that, unable to bear this, you react violently, pulling at the hem of your clothes and shouting your name aloud [to try and affirm your existence]. You tremble, the hairs on your body stand up, and you experience the dissolution of the ten classes of consciousness.[69] At that instant, of the two streams of awareness [one undergoing the experience of dissolution and the other observing this process], think that they are both your own mind; they are but different modes of perception. As you contemplate thus, your thoughts and awarenesses will calm, and your body and mind will rest in their own natural states. When the thought arises spontaneously "Oh, everything is my mind," nonconceptuality dawns in its nakedness.

Therefore, when sickness, malevolent forces, and your own self are examined with the pristine cognition of discriminative awareness, none are found to have ever come into being; this is the unborn dharmakāya. The unborn has no cessation, and this absence of cessation is the unceasing enjoyment buddha body (*saṃbhogakāya*). Between origination and cessation is no abiding, and this absence of abiding is the nonabiding emanation buddha body (*nirmāṇakāya*). That which does not exist in any of the three times is devoid of substantial reality, and this absence of substantial reality is the natural buddha body (*svabhāvakāya*).

View this absence of four resultant buddha bodies—which are separate from the three factors of sickness, malevolent forces, and your own mind—as the [actual] four buddha bodies. In this way you recognize that every conceptualization places the four buddha bodies in your very palms. View every conceptualization as an intimation of ultimate reality. View all illnesses and malevolent forces as embodiments of kindness. This is the "instruction on introducing the four buddha bodies," which presents the transformation of adverse conditions into the path by means of the ultimate awakening mind.

To conclude the practice of the two awakening minds, or as a meditation implicit within it, cultivate the following viewpoint to help sever hopes and fears: "Since this inflicter of harm has led me to train in the two awakening minds, it is placing enlightenment in my very palms. It is thus most kind indeed.

"Furthermore, like a messenger it bears a warning: 'Suffering like the present one results from a cause—a negative, nonvirtuous karma. To avoid suffering in the future, you must purify its cause, the negative karma; forsake all negative acts.' It is therefore kind indeed."

Think, "These perpetrators of harm expose my lack of antidotes, my failure even to notice afflictions arising, and are thereby definitely emanations of my teacher." Thinking thus, view them with joy from the depths of your heart.

Think furthermore, "This one who harms me reveals within this very life the sufferings of a future life in the lower realms—the fruit of my past lives' negative karma. He holds us away from the gaping opening of the lower realms and is therefore most kind indeed."

Reflecting, "If he has benefited me this much, he must definitely be an expression of the enlightened activities of the teachers and the Three Jewels," view the one who harms you as desirable, endearing, and close to your heart. View sickness and other kinds of suffering as having similarly beneficial qualities.

Even if you contract leprosy, reflect, "This will bring the threat of future sufferings to the fore. This life is but a momentary event, and were I not ill with leprosy, my mind would be enmeshed in the chores of this mundane life, leading me to accumulate negative karma. Given that [illnesses and so on] put an abrupt end to this and enable me to encounter Dharma, they help me extract what is most essential from this bodily existence." In this way, view leprosy and other illnesses with heartfelt, uncontrived joy.

Furthermore, think, "Sickness and other sufferings engender true renunciation in me; for without suffering, there can be no true renunciation. Since they definitely help dispel the afflictions of my mind, they help me realize the teachings' intent. So they are most kind indeed!" For it is stated:

With disenchantment, arrogance is dispelled.[70]

Furthermore suffering brings forth compassion, which is the root of the Great Vehicle. For it is stated:

Toward samsaric beings, generate compassion.[71]

Reflect: "Suffering dispels all my suffering and secures all my happiness and therefore brings me benefit." Just as your teachers and preceptors are most kind in conferring vows upon you and giving teachings, sentient beings and harmful elemental forces also help you attain enlightenment. You should therefore view all of them, too, as your spiritual teachers and contemplate their great kindness.

When you learn to train your mind in this manner, all activities of your body, speech, and mind, and everything that appears in the field of your senses will be transformed into the two accumulations. From that point onward, you will have a spiritual practice where nothing goes to waste. It is from here that the three innumerable eons start.

With this, the training in the two awakening minds—the special thoughts—has been presented.

## B. Striving in the dual practice of accumulation and purification, the extraordinary activities

Transforming adverse conditions into the path of enlightenment by means of striving in the twin practices of accumulation and purification—the extraordinary activities—is presented as follows:

**The fourfold practice is the most excellent method.**

When you are suffering, thoughts wishing for happiness arise uncontrollably. Use such moments to motivate you as follows.

1) The first practice is the accumulation of merit: "If you wish for happiness free of suffering, cultivate faith and respect toward the teachers and the Three Jewels, which are the causes of all happiness; gather the accumulations." Think that your suffering admonishes you to think such thoughts. Make extensive offerings to the Three Jewels, offer alms and services to the spiritual community, make torma offerings to the elemental spirits, give charity to ordinary folk, and, making prayers for the cessation of your hopes and fears, offer mandalas and other articles to the teachers and the Three Jewels. Cultivate faith and respect toward them, go for refuge and generate the awakening mind, and make the following appeal with fervent joy: "Since I am ignorant, please care for me in the best way possible." Make the following supplication as well:

> If being sick is best, please make me ill.
> If being cured is best, please restore my health.
> If being dead is best, please make me die.
> If long life is best, please prolong my life.
> If shorter life is best, please shorten my life.
> May all enjoy the fortune of enlightenment.

2) The second practice is the purification of negative karma. Again, imagine that your suffering comes as a messenger, exhorting you, "If you do not desire suffering, abandon the cause, which is negative karma." With this thought, purify negative karma through the four powers.[72] In the presence of the Three Jewels, engage also in the rites requesting forbearance [from them for any shortcomings] as well as engage in the extensive purification rites.

3) The third practice is making offerings to the malevolent forces. Offer torma to the agents of harm. Those who can mentally handle it should also do the following meditation:

Summon in front of you the agent of harm, visualized as a meditation deity, and reflect, "You are kind indeed, for you have led me to the two awakening minds; you have helped me in my quest to find happiness and dispel suffering. I request you further to cause all the sufferings of sentient beings to ripen in my current illness. Please do not depart. Instead stay inside this body of mine and ensure that this sickness is not cured but endures."

Thus joyfully let go of your body and mind, and sever all hopes, fears, and desire for happiness. Without dwelling on sadness, feel a wondrous enthusiasm well up from the depth of your heart.

Those unable to contemplate along these lines should here cultivate loving-kindness and compassion with special emphasis. Reflect, "Through obstructing my work for the benefit of all sentient beings, you will be reborn in the hells in your next life. I will help you with material and spiritual gifts; cease harming me, therefore, and leave." Exhorting thus, confront them with words of truth. Visualizing the agents of harm as deities is like placing an evil person on the seat of a king. Then you will not be able to do them any harm. This is another approach.

4) The fourth practice is offering torma to the Dharma protectors and supplicating them as follows: "Please ensure that no

obstacles arise in my meditative practice. Remember the promises and the solemn oaths you have taken in the presence of the buddhas."

Train with effort in this way in these four practices—(1) making offerings to the deities and the spiritual teachers and supplicating them, (2) purifying your negative karma, (3) making offerings to the malevolent forces, and (4) making offerings to the Dharma protectors.

Having now presented the practice of taking adverse conditions onto the path, the following presents the yoga of in-between sessions:

### Relate whatever you can to meditation right now.

When adverse circumstances strike unexpectedly, train in the two awakening minds right there and then. For instance, if you are struck with leprosy or a severe infection, if you are lynched, beaten, robbed, or attacked with weapons, or if you simply fail to fulfill your desires (due to harms from inanimate forces or acute, unbearable pain), think how the vast universe contains infinite cases like your own, and generate compassion for those. As you mentally take all of these upon your own suffering in one fell swoop, imagine your suffering increases to such intensity that your heart feels it will break.

Following this, reflect, "This inflicter of harm has been my spiritual teacher for training in the awakening mind and the practice of forbearance, and has thus been most kind to me." The moment you see these sufferings in others, right there and then take them upon yourself. Also when intense, unbearable afflictions arise in others due to their attachment and anger, contemplate as before and heap them upon yourself. After this imagine all other beings as free of both suffering and its causes and enjoying happiness.

Langri Thangpa once said, "All of what is called 'transforming adverse conditions into enlightenment' entails the cessation of hopes and fears. So long as these two do not cease, you cannot take adverse conditions onto the path. Even if eventually you happened to be led to the path that is free of hopes and fears, to train in the differentiation of enemy and friend at that time would be like trying to straighten a crooked tree."[73]

## IV. Presentation of a lifetime's practice in summary

The fourth point, the presentation of a lifetime's practice in summary, is presented in the following:

> **In brief the essence of instruction is this:**
> **Apply yourself to the five powers.**

The yogi of this teaching should engage in all mind training by means of a condensed practice of the five powers.

1) First is the *power of propelling intention*. "From now until my full enlightenment, I will never be divorced from the two awakening minds, and I will not allow my mind training to lose its continuity. From now until my death, I will never part from the two awakening minds." Repeat the same resolve in terms of "this year" and "this month," and so on. Repeatedly propel your thoughts in this way with great force.

2) The *power of acquaintance* refers to cultivating the two awakening minds at all times, free of distraction.

3) The *power of positive seeds* means striving, during the periods in between formal sitting sessions, in virtuous activities—such as engaging in the ten spiritual practices,[74] without any interruption and through whatever medium is most convenient, whether it is your body or your wealth—in order to engen-

der those experiences of this mind training teaching that have not yet arisen and enhance those already arisen.

4) The *power of eradication* is the actual eradication of self-grasping. How long have you wandered in cyclic existence in general and in the three lower realms in particular? This is brought about by cherishing your self and desiring its happiness. Even within this life, all undesirable events—inability to maintain a relationship with your partner, lack of integrity in your promises and vows, and an absence of interest in cultivating the spiritual realizations, from the rarity of human existence to no-self—all are due to cherishing your self and desiring its happiness. Every one of your defects is therefore contingent upon this. With the thought "From here on I will never seek the self's welfare for even a single instant; instead, I must totally eliminate this," view self-cherishing in this manner and regard it as the enemy.

5) The *power of aspirational prayer* is this. Upon completing any virtuous act, make the following aspiration: "From this moment until I have attained buddhahood, throughout all my lives, may I never be divorced from the two awakening minds, and may I instead train in them. May I know how to take all circumstances that befall me, whether positive or adverse, into this training." Then make offerings to the teachers and the Three Jewels, and offer a torma to the Dharma protectors and the elemental spirits, supplicating them thus: "Help me so that I am never divorced from the two awakening minds throughout all my lives. Help me to meet sublime teachers who reveal this teaching." This, the master said, is a teaching that folds everything into a single utterance of *hūṃ*.

> As Mahayana's transference method is
> the five powers alone, their practice is vital.

Thus when those who have trained their minds throughout their entire lives contract a fatal illness and become aware of their imminent death, they must apply this very mind training teaching as the time-of-death instruction and effect the transition while engaged in such practice. Practices such as tantra cannot be practiced at this juncture; they should go through the transition by means of the five powers alone.

1) First undertake the practice of the power of *positive seeds*.[75] To do this, you offer your belongings to the teachers and the Three Jewels as the gifts of the deceased.[76] It is inappropriate to give these belongings to beings who might be your objects of clinging. Prepare so that even in your aftermath your possessions do not become conditions for accumulating negative karma. Make excellent offerings to those worthy of veneration. It is inappropriate to offer only tokens of your belongings to those who are embodiments of kindness.[77] Then, without any attachment to your possessions of this life, generate a fearless attitude with regard to your future life.

2) The power of *aspirational prayer* is as follows. Lay out an excellent array of offerings in the presence of the Three Jewels, request forbearance for your shortcomings, and declare and purify your negative karma. Review as well the pledges you have taken, such as that of going for refuge. Then make offerings to the Three Jewels, offer tormas to the Dharma protectors, and make this fervent request to be led to the threshold of the path: "Bless me so that in the intermediate state and the next life I will remember the two awakening minds and engage in their practice. Help me to encounter sublime teachers who reveal this teaching. Lead me to the beginning of my path of happiness. Today I place my hope in you." Then invoke the following aspirations again and again: "May I train in the two awakening minds during the intermediate state; may I train in the two awakening minds through-

out all lives; may I meet sublime teachers who reveal this teaching."

3) The power of *eradication* is as follows. "That which grasps at self and 'I' has made me suffer since beginningless time and has also caused my present suffering. So long as I am not divorced from this, no happiness can arise. How have I allowed it to ruin me? This happened because I have assumed a physical body. So I will definitely not assume a physical body in the intermediate state. I will allow my mind to fade into space." Reflecting in this manner repeatedly, eradicate self-grasping.

4) Next is the power of *propelling intention*. "In the past I enhanced the two awakening minds so that their continuity was not interrupted. I will now recollect the two awakening minds during the intermediate state and engage in their training." Repeatedly reflect and recollect along these lines.

5) As for the power of *acquaintance*, the key is to first train uninterruptedly in the awakening mind.

Then, as you approach the moment of death, lie down on your right and, placing your right hand on your cheek, block the right nostril with your little finger, and breathe through the left nostril. This is transference in terms of your conduct.

Then, preceded by loving-kindness, train in the dual practice of giving and taking on the basis of your in- and out-breaths. While in this state, engage in the practice of ultimate awakening mind thus, contemplating, "Everything that shares the nature of samsara and nirvana has its root in the deluded mind. As for the mind, it never deviates from its primordial nature of dharmakāya." Reflect how, in reality, even what is called death has no existence. Combine these two contemplations, engage in their practice, and die while in that mindstate.

If you are unable to do this, then arouse the true nature of samsara and nirvana that is free of rejection and affirmation within the expanse of the ever-present innate dharmakāya, which is the uncontrived mind itself. Release your mind restfully in the ultimate expanse and place it upon the mind's ultimate nature, which is devoid of transference.[78] Then, even if you are unable to die [in tune with the meditative state] because of temporarily losing your mindfulness, you will still die with the instruction appropriate for the moment of death. Although numerous celebrated moment-of-death instructions exist, the master said nothing is more amazing than this [instruction presented here].

With these, the complete aspects of the path have been presented without omission.

## V. Presentation of the measure of having trained the mind

The fifth point, the measure of having trained the mind, is presented by the following:

### The intent of all teachings converges on a single point.

The scriptures and the treatises were taught for the purpose of overcoming self-grasping; thus there is no target for the trio of study, reflection, and meditation to destroy other than this. When examined, the selfhood of persons is as nonexistent as the horns of a rabbit; nevertheless it has made us suffer since beginningless time. Observe and analyze whether all your endeavors of body, speech, and mind are directed toward reinforcing your self-grasping or bringing its downfall. If they are reinforcing it, you are striving solely out of the eight mundane concerns and for the pursuit of greatness in this life. If this is the case, then even if you are observing ethical discipline with dedication, you have erred with regard to your paternal spiritual lineage. Even if you are training the mind through study, reflection, and meditation, your practice has gone awry.

On the other had, if your endeavors are toppling self-grasping, you are achieving the true purpose of industrious ethical discipline and you are training the mind skillfully. In this way, by fostering genuine mind-training realizations in your mind, you can likewise attain the full measure of Dharma practice. Since this is a benchmark for determining whether a Dharma practice has truly become a Dharma practice, the master said, this is the long bar of a scale on which the practitioner is weighed. Learn how to turn all your endeavors of body, speech, and mind into antidotes to self-grasping.

**Of the two witnesses uphold the principal one.**

People might say of you, "This brother's heart has become softened, like a piece of wool that has been washed. Genuine spiritual practice has arisen in him. 'True Dharma practitioner' refers to all who are like him." Not being disapproved of by those who are reputedly sublime is a form of witness. But this should not be the principal one. Why? Others may praise you when they observe one or two good actions or when you do a few things that please them, but other people cannot fully penetrate your depths.

What, then, is the principal witness? It is avoiding your own scorn. Feel that, even if you were to die this evening, you could have done nothing more; you have striven to the best of your capacity with faith, intelligence, and perseverance, regardless of how weak these may have been, such that your guts fill with air, and blood and water gush forth [within your veins].[79] At that point you have attained a qualified stage of meditative practice. Therefore hold the principal witness to be this fact of not becoming the object of your own scorn.

**Cultivate constantly the joyful mind alone.**

This line suggests that, having trained your mind and tasted the flavor of true Dharma practice, no matter what adverse circumstances befall you, you experience no disturbance within, for you immediately think: "I can cultivate its remedy, the two awakening minds." Remaining unassailed in such a manner is another measure of having trained your mind.

In the same vein, regarding the four desirable things and four undesirable things in the world, when you train the mind by focusing on the four undesirable things,[80] everything becomes desirable. You will find no precipitous terrain or obstructions, and thus your mind will always be filled with joy, and the edifice [of your Dharma practice] will not crumble. This too is a measure of having trained the mind.

Again, when you have trained the mind in the dual practice of giving and taking, then whatever suffering afflicts your body and mind, you will spontaneously have the thought, "Now, my theft from others in the past has its consequence," and you will once again experience extraordinary joy. In brief, whatever undesirable events occur, if they are conducive for training your mind and cause no disquiet, this is the measure of having trained the mind. At that point your remedy has reached its true depth.

**If this can be done even when distracted, you are trained.**

Just as a skilled rider does not fall when the horse rears suddenly, a trained mind spontaneously applies antidotes when adversities arise unexpectedly, such as unanticipated criticism and insults. If these become conducive to the awakening mind, and if you do not fall prey to adversities, your mind is trained.

Furthermore, cultivate the thought, "The time of my death is unknown, and were it to come suddenly, my sole recourse would be this practice. This is true Dharma; wonderful indeed is my path!" In this way, make sure you fortify your mind so that no matter when you die, you do so joyfully and with palpable warmth within.

If you have these signs of being trained, illnesses and demons will enhance your realizations. This doesn't mean that you need not train your mind further. This merely presents the measure of when the remedy has been applied fully.

## VI. Presentation of the commitments of mind training

### Train constantly in the three general points.

This line expresses that (1) your mind training should not contravene your pledges, (2) your mind training should not become ostentatious, and (3) your mind training should not be biased.

1) The first means relinquishing all behaviors that disregard the law of karma and its results. This includes ignoring the minor precepts with the assertion "Since I am training the mind, nothing can harm me" and behaving in ways that contradict general Dharma conduct, saying, "If I have this mind training, I don't need anything else." Engage in mind training with your thoughts, while in your actions observe, in a pure way, all the pledges and commitments you have taken, from the Vinaya up to the Vajrayana. Make sure your practice and everyday conduct accord with and can withstand close scrutiny when judged against the scriptures.

2) The second point means discarding such ostentatious behaviors as sleeping in dangerous places, felling harmful trees,[81] visiting areas where you may contract contagious diseases, associating with people whose commitments have lapsed, with lepers, or with those possessed by demons. Do not act contrary to the Kadampa's way of life, a great tradition

that has been established by Geshé Dromtönpa at Radreng. Practice instead as if lifting all four corners of square cloth. Shawopa has said: "Examine where you might go astray. You have erred when your spiritual practice becomes obnoxious." Forsake consorting with those with degenerated commitments or morality or who commit negative acts, and make sure your conduct does not become ostentatious.

3) The third point, not being biased, refers to the following. Some practitioners can tolerate harms from humans but not from nonhumans; they are obsessed with demonic harms. For others the reverse is true. Some practitioners are respectful toward important people but bully the weak. Some are affectionate toward their family but hostile toward outsiders. Others train their mind in relation to sentient beings but not in relation to elemental spirits. These attitudes are all biased. Train your mind to be free of such discriminations.

**Transform your attitudes but remain as you are.**

While practicing the exchange of self and others and reflecting on this yoga—not divorced from it for even a single instant in your thought or in your physical and verbal conduct—you must nonetheless maintain your conduct the way it was before, with no radical shift. For instance, do not recite [mind training sayings to show off] in others' presence, but strive to conform with others. Maintain your normal level of spiritual activity, and leave your external behaviors unchanged. Some people, after hearing the teaching, become fickle, discarding their past manner and practices. This is tantamount to forsaking your past, which is extremely inappropriate. Since it is taught that your mind training should be discreet yet powerful, ripen your mind without others noticing.

### Do not speak of the defects of others.

This states that you should never speak of others' defects— neither their worldly defects, for instance by saying "that blind person," nor their spiritual defects, for instance by saying "that morally degenerate person."

### Do not reflect on others' shortcomings.

It is inappropriate to ruminate on the shortcomings of sentient beings in general and particularly of those who have entered the monastic order, especially your fellow practitioners. At minimum, you should be joyful toward them, for you are training the mind. Even if you happen to feel that certain associates may be ill chosen, since you are training the mind, contemplating others' shortcomings is inappropriate. If you lapse and find yourself noticing another's shortcoming, think, "This is my own deluded perception; no such flaw exists in them. All sentient beings are endowed with the essence that shares the Buddha's own nature." Reflect in this manner and judge this perception to be your own flaw.

### Discard all expectations of reward.

Discard all expectations, such as admiration for your mind training; material gifts, services, and fame; protection from harm caused by nonhumans in this and future lives; the attainment of a joyful human or heavenly existence; and the attainment of nirvana. Ensure that you have no expectation even of buddhahood for your own sake. Do not harbor impatience and excessive hope even for the meditative qualities, for were the demons to learn of this, they could create obstacles. Even if you exert strong effort with no ebbing of interest for a long time but still get no results, do not get discouraged.

**Discard poisonous food.**

[Poisonous food is] self-interest harbored in the depths of your heart. Never fail to perceive self-grasping as the enemy, nor fail to release self-cherishing and the thoughts that grasp at the substantial reality of things. These make everything you do into a cause of cyclic existence, binding you within cyclic existence and giving rise to suffering. Since these are all like poisonous food, you must discard them.

**Do not maintain [inappropriate] loyalty.**

This means you should not refrain from condemning acts of injustice committed by others while holding them accountable [out of a misplaced sense of loyalty].

**Do not torment with malicious banter.**

Whatever tasks befall you, do not indulge in malicious jibes that tear at others' hearts or cause them to lose their composure. Regardless of their culpability, avoid insulting and speaking harshly to others—whether close or distant, good or bad.

**Do not lie in ambush.**

Do not harbor vengeance for a wrong done to you, waiting for an opportune moment to retaliate.

**Do not strike at the heart.**

Toward both humans and nonhumans, avoid delving into their weaknesses. With nonhumans, for instance, avoid uttering fierce life-extracting mantras; and in the case of humans, avoid exposing their moral lapses, for instance, in situations where many people are around.

**Do not place the load of a dzo onto an ox.**

Avoid such negative behavior as attempting, by devious means, to shift blame and liabilities onto others that would otherwise fall on you.

**Do not sprint to win a race.**

Avoid such behavior as attempting, through unbecoming conduct and other means, to transfer the ownership of commonly owned objects to yourself. You should not be in a state of craving when you die, and since the "other shore" will arise in any case because of karma, it is far more joyful to let go with a sense of ease, the master said.

**Do not abuse this [practice] as a rite.**

There is no qualitative difference between someone who, seeking long-term well-being, accepts certain loss in the interim and someone who engages in mind training as a ritual with the long-term motivation to conquer demonic harms. Therefore avoid behavior such as this that fails to root out the jaundice of self-centeredness from its depth. Some practitioners seem to think that mind training practice is beneficial for such a result or purpose. If this is true, there is no real difference between practicing mind training and engaging in shamanistic rites. To be called Dharma practice, mind training must become an antidote to afflictions and false conceptualization.

### Do not turn the gods into demons.

When displeased, the worldly gods cause harm. The gods are supposed to be beneficial in general; so if they cause harm, they then become demons. Similarly, mind training is supposed to subdue self-grasping. Avoid, therefore, becoming inflated by its practice and generating conceited thoughts such as, "I am an excellent practitioner of mind training; others lack this spiritual practice." Avoid ridiculing and insulting others out of a sense of superiority. If you strengthen your grasping at the self-existence of phenomena, your practice becomes an endeavor of the enemy. It becomes the act of allowing a thief to escape into the forest while tracking his footprints on a rocky mountain. Avoid all such conduct, and by defaming self-grasping, ensure that the medicine is applied right where the illness is. Comport yourself as the lowest of the low among the servants of all sentient beings.

### Do not seek misery as a means to happiness.

This means not drawing personal gratification from others' miseries. Do not, for example, harbor thoughts such as, "If my spouse or this particular friend dies, there will then be no other family member left [so I will inherit everything]," "If the wealthy benefactor becomes ill or dies, I will have the opportunity to accumulate merit and roots of virtue," "If my meditator colleague of this region dies, I alone will have the opportunity to accumulate merit," and "If this enemy dies, I will enjoy happiness." The master said that since sentient beings experience their own individual merits, due to karma you will find enemies and friends no matter where you go.

## VII. Presentation of the precepts of mind training

Since your mind training will not degenerate but will instead be enhanced to progressively higher levels if you put the following teachings into practice, strive in them.

**Accomplish all yogas through a single means.**

Other spiritual practices have their own particular dietary requirements, modes of conduct, and so on, in addition to their yogic practices. For those like you who have entered the door of mind training, however, solely keeping in mind this mind training advice is sufficient to ensure all other practices, such as those pertaining to food. So you should engage in this practice.

**Overcome all errors through a single means.**

Some who are under Māra's influence fail to develop confidence in this spiritual practice. They experience the false perceptions of misguided meditation practice, with thoughts like: "Since I began practicing mind training, illnesses have increased, harms from demons have increased, people have become more hostile, and afflictions such as self-grasping have increased as well." Based on such thoughts, or for no particular reason, they lose enthusiasm for mind training and are in danger of turning away. If this happens to you, become aware of it right there and then and think, "A misguided meditative practice has arisen in me." With a second thought, reflect, "There must be many like me in the universe whose thoughts have deviated from true Dharma practice," and take all of these deviations upon yourself and offer your body, wealth, and virtues to others. Imagine that because of this, the thoughts of those others turn toward the Dharma, and these others enter the unmistaken path.

**There are two tasks—one at the start and one
at the end.**

In the morning, after getting up, set forth the thought,
"Throughout this day I will be sure to avoid becoming tainted
by the clinging of self-cherishing. I will make sure my thoughts
cherishing others do not degenerate." Then, during the day,
remain sustained by the vigilance that accompanies everyday
activity.

When going to bed at night, while in the meditative absorption "lion's majestic pose," sequentially review the day by recall-
ing, "First I did this, then I did that, and so on." If you detect
any transgression, it is stated, "At that instant enumerate your
flaws / and recall your teacher's instructions."[82] Then cultivate
the following thought: "Isn't it amazing that there are people
like me who waste their precious human existence and bring
harm upon themselves!" Thinking thus, appeal for forbearance, declare and purify your negative karma, and cultivate the
resolve to forsake this in the future. If you have not committed
any transgression, then rejoice, thinking, "I have indeed made
my human existence meaningful." Dedicate the virtues toward
the aspiration to realize this practice in your mental continuum. Also make the aspiration prayer, "May I never be divorced
from the two awakening minds throughout all my lives."

**Whichever of the two arises, be patient.**

If you suddenly come into a great fortune, do not become arrogant or become attached to it; make sure you do not fall prey to
the eight mundane concerns. Take this good fortune as a basis
for your Dharma practice. Some people who attract followers
and material gifts become conceited by this; they then despise

others and do whatever comes to mind. You must discard such behavior.

Likewise, if you experience misfortune such that the only thing that seems beneath you is the water [flowing under a bridge], do not become depressed or demoralized, wondering how "such an unfortunate person like me" could exist. Do not be so downcast you are incapable of training the mind. Instead reflect, "Compared to the disparity in degree and intensity between the happiness of the higher realms and the suffering of the lower realms, the disparity between pleasant and unpleasant human states is not so immense. So, without distracting myself further, I will focus on my spiritual practices." For it is taught:

> Even if you are prosperous like the gods,
> Pray do not be conceited.
> Even if you become as destitute as a hungry ghost,
> Pray do not be disheartened.[83]

**Guard the two even at the cost of your life.**

These are (1) the precepts and commitments presented in the teachings in general and (2) the commitments of this particular mind training teaching, such as "Do not speak of the defects [of others]." Since even the mundane happiness of this present life will elude you if these two commitments become degenerate, hold them more dearly than your life.

**Train in the three difficult challenges.**

When eliminating the afflictions, in the beginning it can be difficult to remember the antidotes, in the middle it can be difficult to overcome the afflictions, and at the end it can be difficult to eradicate the continuum of the afflictions. Therefore make sure you accomplish these three without great difficulty. To train, in the morning put on the armor with respect to all three stages. When the afflictions actually arise, recall their antidotes, counter them, and cultivate the resolve, "From here on I will not allow the afflictions to arise in my mind."

**Adopt the three principal conditions.**

(1) There should be a qualified spiritual teacher who possesses the pith instructions and is endowed with higher realizations. The bond [between the teacher and you] should be so close that no dog can come between, and the teacher should be pleased with you. (2) Your state of mind should be such that [many realizations have arisen]—from [the rarity of] precious human existence to [the understanding of] no-self—and these should have arisen just as contemplated or as taught by your teacher. (3) Conditions conducive to Dharma practice must be gathered—such as faith, intelligence, joyous effort, a strong sense of disenchantment, food and clothing, and other necessities.

Since these three are the principal conditions of Dharma practice, if you possess them, rejoice and strive diligently to enhance them. If you do not possess them, contemplate: "How sad! The vast expanse of the universe must contain countless others like me who lack these three factors and have failed in their Dharma practice." Thinking thus, take upon yourself all their deficiencies. As you offer your body and so on to them, imagine they obtain the three conditions and that all experience the Great Vehicle.

**Contemplate the three that are free of degeneration.**

Since all the attainments of the Mahayana depend upon the student's faith and respect [toward his or her teacher], make sure you are never divorced at any time from the perception of your teacher as a buddha. In this manner, make sure that your faith and respect toward your spiritual teacher remain undiminished. Furthermore, with the thought "This mind training teaching represents the quintessence of Mahayana and is like a potent seed of buddhahood," engage in this incomparable practice. Thus make sure your enthusiasm for mind training remains undiminished. As for the pledges of the Great and Lesser vehicles you have taken, you should, by sailing the great ship of shame and conscientiousness, which are the true antidotes, learn to guard them undiminished, not tainted by even the slightest infractions.

**Be endowed with the three inseparable factors.**

Make sure that your body is never divorced from such virtuous acts as offering services to your spiritual teachers, making offerings to the Three Jewels, offering torma cakes to the Dharma protectors and the elemental spirits, making prostrations, performing circumambulation, and so on. Make sure that your speech is never divorced from such virtuous acts as reciting verses on taking refuge, repeating mantras, and doing recitations. Make sure that your mind is never divorced from the two awakening minds and is endowed with inconceivable courage to vanquish all the conceptualizing afflictions, such as self-cherishing. In brief, make sure your body, speech, and mind are never divorced from virtuous activity at all times.

**Train constantly toward the chosen objects.**

It is said that the tendency to get angry and vengeful toward enemies and adversaries right to their faces is exacerbated by frequent interactions. Thus, from one angle, there is a real risk of losing your mind training in relation to those who harbor ill-will against you even though you have caused them no harm, and those you find unpleasant even though they harbor no ill-will toward you. Therefore single these people out for special focus, and train your mind by perceiving them as parts of your own heart. Furthermore, because your spiritual teachers, parents, and bodhisattvas are objects of special significance—the fruitional effects are inconceivably grave if you accumulate negative karma in relation to them—single them out [for special focus] and engage in the training.

### Do not depend on other conditions.

To engage in other spiritual practices, you have to gather various favorable conditions, such as food, clothing, and so on; you also need to have good health, access to water that is suited to your body, and no excessive disturbances from humans and nonhumans alike. The practice of mind training, in contrast, does not depend on such conditions. Since the very absence of favorable conditions is itself a resource for this spiritual practice, today take all of these as the ripening of meritorious karma and as factors conducive to mind training.

### Engage in the principal practices right now.

Since beginningless time you have roamed the three lower realms of existence as if they were your ancestral home. Today, at this juncture, when you have obtained the human existence of leisure and opportunity that is so rarely found in even a billion eons, instead of making all kinds of plans for this life, it is more important to engage in Dharma practice that aims for the welfare of future lives. Of the two aspects of Dharma, exposition and practice, the latter is more important. Compared to all other meditative practices, the practice of training in the awakening mind is more important. Compared to training the mind by applying the twin paddles of scripture and reasoning, persistently training in applying the appropriate antidotes on the basis of your teacher's pith instructions is more important. Compared to other activities, training by remaining seated on your cushion is more important. Compared to avoiding the objects of your afflictions, probing within is more important. It is critical that you train in these points.

### Do not apply misplaced understanding.

This refers to the avoidance of six misplaced understandings. If, instead of enduring the hardships entailed in Dharma practice, you endure difficulties when seeking the objects of your desire, nurturing your friends, and subduing your foes—this is *misplaced endurance*. If, instead of aspiring to purify your negative karma as much as you can, accumulate merit as much as you can, and transform your thoughts as much as you can, you view the excellences of this life as admirable qualities and aspire to them—this is *misplaced aspiration*. If, instead of savoring your experience of the Dharma through striving in learning, reflection, and meditation, you savor the taste of sensual desire and pursue it and you dwell on and relish memories of past sexual experiences and triumphs over enemies—this is *misplaced savoring*. If, instead of cultivating compassion for those caught in suffering and its causes, you feel compassion for those who suffer in pursuit of the ascetic life and meditation—this is *misplaced compassion*. If, instead of cultivating dedication to the privilege of practicing Dharma, you have a sense of dedication to such endeavors as accumulating material wealth, nurturing friends, and pursuing mundane greatness—this is *misplaced dedication*. If, instead of rejoicing in those—from the buddhas to the sentient beings—who engage in virtue and enjoy its fruit, happiness, you rejoice when misfortune and disaster befall your adversaries—this is *misplaced rejoicing*. You should relate to these six misplaced understandings with appropriate avoidance and affirmation.

### Do not be sporadic.

At times you practice mind training while at others you engage in mantra repetitions; on some occasions you forsake both, yet on other occasions you guard both. Relinquish such a sporadic approach. Forsake also such sporadic approaches as sometimes making plans for this mundane life and increasing negative karma and afflictions and sometimes engaging in Dharma practice for the sake of your future life. Without being sporadic, engage in Dharma practice with single-pointed dedication. In particular, practice mind training, for mind training is the innermost essence of Dharma practice.

### Train with decisiveness.

When a minor nerve is damaged, you treat it by cutting it clean. In the same way, when you engage in the training of mind, do not remain hesitant but direct your entire mind. You should remain resolute in your decision and train with no hesitation. Avoid such dilettantish attitudes as, "First I will check to see if mind training is beneficial; if not, I will recite mantras." This indicates that you have failed to let go of yearning for [self-centered] happiness; this kind of practice can't even overcome sickness and malevolent possessions.

**Be released through the two: investigation and close analysis.**

First investigate which affliction is most dominant in your mind and earnestly apply its specific antidote, striving hard to subdue the affliction. Then analyze the way deluded mental projections arise in relation to the objects that act as their bases. By applying the antidotes, you reduce the force of the afflictions or prevent their arising. By repeatedly thinking, "From here on I will never allow my mindstream to be tainted by these afflictions," you cultivate familiarity with the protective armor for the future. Thus, with these twin methods for applying antidotes to past and future [afflictions], strive diligently to eliminate the afflictions.[84]

**Do not boast of your good deeds.[85]**

Don't be boastful and arrogant toward others on any grounds, suggesting, for example, that another person is indebted to you, or that you engage in certain spiritual practices, or that you are learned, or that you are industrious in your ethical discipline, or that you are great, or that your family lineage is excellent. Radrengpa has said, "Don't place too much hope in humans; supplicate the gods instead."[86] In any case, if you have correctly distinguished between enemy and friend, you understand everyone to be a friend. Then even when you work for others' welfare, the jaundice of self-centeredness does not arise. Instead you recognize all such tasks as obligations, so boastfulness toward others simply does not occur. When that happens, your mind has become trained.

**Do not be ill-tempered.**

Whatever others may have done to you in the past, such as humiliating you or verbally abusing you, the blame lies within you. Do not react to others with twisted facial expressions or abusive words. Even with your mind, restrain yourself from ill-temperedness. Because your Dharma practice has not yet become an antidote to self-grasping, your resilience is at present weak, and your ill temper makes you volatile. Since such behavior makes your Dharma practice ineffective, ensure that your practice becomes an antidote to self-grasping.

**Do not be fickle.**

Don't respond erratically to situations because of your ever-changing moods. This causes great inconvenience to your companions and must therefore be relinquished.

**Do not be boisterous.**

Avoid seeking fame and praise through expressions of gratitude for assistance you may have rendered others or benefits you may have brought them. In brief, do not desire even to hear compliments for help or assistance rendered to others.

In this manner you should train, your entire life, in the two awakening minds both through meditation sessions and through practice in the periods between sessions. There will then be no basis for dispute and no reason for conflict with the gods, demons, or fellow humans. By putting the gods at peace, making the serpentine nāgas tranquil, and keeping everyone happy as best as possible, when your last breath approaches, you will experience the beginning of true happiness, and you will turn your back on misery and travel from light to light, from joy to joy.

The effects or benefits of these spiritual practices are presented in the following:

**Through this proliferation of the five degenerations
transform [every event] into the path of enlightenment.**

Generally speaking, the teaching of Buddha Śākyamuni
emerged in an era when the five degenerations were on the rise.
In particular, it has emerged during this present age, the era of
the last five-hundred-year cycle, when the types of degeneration are even more severe than the five degenerations. Because
of this, sentient beings's thoughts are only afflictions, their
actions only negative karma. They relish others' suffering and
feel anguished at others' good fortune. Thus with all three
doors—body, speech, and mind—sentient beings indulge only
in deeds that are harmful to others. It is therefore an era when
[harmful] sentient beings have gathered.

Furthermore, those nonhuman agents that admire the positive white force have departed to the pure realms to benefit the
bodhisattvas, whereas the strength and force of those who
admire the dark side have increased. Because of this, misfortunes plague sentient beings.

Today, therefore, a multitude of adverse conditions cause all
kinds of suffering for sentient beings, and myriad obstacles particularly befall those who put the doctrine into practice. So at
this time, when adverse conditions compete to form a thicket,
if you do not train in this spiritual practice, though you may
enter other systems of practice, you will fail to succeed in
Dharma practice. On the other hand, if you enter this practice
and strive in it, you will transform all adverse conditions into
factors conducive for training on the path to enlightenment.

As for other benefits, a year's pursuit of virtuous activities
during this age—when the teaching of the Buddha faces pernicious threats—will help you accomplish the accumulations better than eons pursuing virtue in the pure realms. Therefore,
those truly capable of training the mind are invulnerable to the

spread of the five degenerations and remain content. If you know how to train the mind, even your body, the body of a mind training yogi, is known as the "city that is a fount of joy." For all happiness—of this and future lives, of self and others—comes about on the basis of this very body.

Strive therefore by concentrating all your efforts in this endeavor. And if you make sure that the teachings are integrated with your mind—that the rule of Dharma is established as firmly as a stake driven through your heart—and that you experience the taste of Dharma, before long you will attain the perfect state, wherein the complete aims of self and others are accomplished. Thus said the master.

To illustrate these points definitively, the author himself wrote the following lines:

> **Because of my numerous aspirations,**
> **I have defied the tragic tale of suffering**
> **and have taken instructions to subdue self-grasping.**
> **Now, even if death comes, I have no regrets.**

These words were uttered as an expression of joy by the highly accomplished yogi Chekawa, who, having presented the method of practice, arrived at a decisively settled state of mind following a clear discrimination between enemy and friend.

### Colophon

These words of my teacher, an ocean of goodness delighting
  everyone:
Through the merit of compiling them with a wish to
  help others,
may the giant elephant of mind training carry all beings
and demolish the solid mountain of egoistic view.

As the rays of your fame pervade all directions,
like a magnet attracting all metal objects,
stirred by your fame, your disciples remain in your presence;
they've beheld your face so rare and have accomplished
   great aims.

In the sky of the exalted mind of Serlingpa's lineage,
though the sun of mind training still shines brilliantly,
it is now obscured by clouds of negative conceptualization;
the line between gold and worn-out brass has become blurred.

O, those who wish to relinquish the sufferings of self
   and others,
forsake the inferior paths described as incomplete
and enter this horse-drawn carriage path of the Conqueror's
   supreme children.

How can anyone hope to become enlightened without this?
A distillation of all scriptures,
this innermost essence of Kadam is most wondrous!

*Sarva śubham*

# EIGHT VERSES

AMONG THE FIRST indigenious Tibetan works on mind training to capture the heart of spiritual aspirants in the land of snows is undoubtedly the beautifully concise and moving verse text known as *Eight Verses on Mind Training*. Sometimes referred to also as *Langthangpa's Eight Verses*, the thirty-two lines of this short work encapsulate powerfully the depth of the altruistic ideal and commitment of a spiritual aspirant who is dedicated to the pursuit of bringing about the ultimate welfare of all sentient beings.

Beginning with the critical question of how to view others with a sense of deep gratitude, the text plunges immediately into the heart of the matter—namely, the challenge of how to transform our habitual self-centeredness into a standpoint of valuing and cherishing the welfare of others.

In stanza 2, the author then deals with the more specific question of how to implement this principle of cherishing others' welfare. A key to this, we are told, lies in adopting an appropriate outlook toward self and others, an outlook that shuns viewing others as somehow inferior.

Stanza 3 tells us that, in order for us mind training practioners to put our spiritual ideals into practice, we need first and foremost to find a way to deal with the perennial challenge posed by our habitual afflictive states of mind. Here, Langri Thangpa emphasizes the need to cultivate and apply in our thoughts and behavior faculties such as mindfulness, greater self-awareness, and heedfulness.

In stanzas 4, 5, and 6, this advice on how to deal with our afflictions is taken further, with special attention given to particular types of people: beings of unpleasant character, those oppressed with negativity, those who treat us wrongly for no good reason, and finally those who disappoint us—people, in other words, who trigger powerful negative reactions in us. These lines clearly resonate with Śāntideva's famous advice to view our enemies as spiritual teachers, for they provide us the rare opportunity to practice the virtue of patience, or forbearance.

Stanza 7 sums up the key principle of mind training— transforming of our thoughts, attitudes, and behaviors to be more other-regarding and altruistic. This is done on the basis of presenting the contemplative practice of *tonglen* (giving and taking), which entails mentally taking upon ourselves all the sufferings of others and their causes, while offering to others our happiness and its causes.

Finally, in stanza 8, we find the instruction on how to ensure that all of the above spiritual exercises do not become sullied by the motives and underlying states of mind driven by self-centered, mundane concerns. The exercises should be grounded instead in an understanding of the deeper nature of reality, so that, finally, free from clinging, we attain genuine freedom from bondage.

In this volume, we provide two slightly different versions of the famed eight verses. First is the "original" version that is embedded in Chekawa's commentary, while the second can be referred to as the "revised" version. The primary difference lies, in the original Tibetan, in the key verb at the end of each stanza. In the original text, we find the phrase "I will train myself to" in relation to practices outlined in each of the eight stanzas. In contrast, the revised version has the phrase "May I," thus transforming the contents of each stanza into a prayer of aspiration rather than a vow to practice. This change was introduced in the twelfth century, soon after the composition of the text, by Sangchenpa. Since the later, revised version is used by all Tibetan teachers today, we have provided this popular version of the text as well.

Langri Thangpa (1054–1123), whose personal name was Dorjé Sengé, was a senior disciple of the Kadam master Potowa Rinchen Sal (1031–1105), one of the three Kadam brothers. He founded Langthang Monastery in Phenpo in central southern Tibet in 1093, which is said to have attracted around two thousand monks during his own lifetime. As noted in my general introduction, Langri Thangpa is famed for the depth of his constant contemplation of the sufferings of all sentient beings, such that he would often be seen with tears rolling down his face. According to the earliest sources, it is Langri Thangpa who first introduced the tradition of sharing the mind training teachings with a wider audience as opposed to the smaller teacher-to-pupil transmission. Langri Thangpa's principal student was Shawo Gangpa, and it is said that the Kagyü master Phakmo Drupa (1110–70) also received teachings from Langri Thangpa.

The commentary on the eight verses featured in this volume is, to date, the earliest known exposition of Langri Thangpa's *Eight Verses*. Although the colophon of the text explicitly states Master Chekawa, the person who composed the well-known *Seven-Point Mind Training*, to be its author, the work opens with the statement, in honorific Tibetan, about how the spiritual mentor Chekawa received the instruction on the eight verses from the Kadam master Chakshingwa. Furthermore, the commentary carries the title *Eight Verses on Mind Training Together with the Story of Its Origin*, which suggests that at least the opening section of the text was added by a later editor.

Given the brevity of the root text of the eight verses, the most important contribution of this commentary is the way it grounds the instructions presented by Langri Thangpa within the context of scriptural sources and illuminates the thought process, or rationale, underlying each of the practices. For example, the commentary links the mind training instructions to specific verses from Śāntideva's *Guide to the Bodhisattva's Way of Life*, a seminal basis for the development of *lojong* teachings, as well as lines from other important classical Indian Buddhist texts, such as Nāgārjuna's *Precious Garland*. In doing so, Chekawa enables us, the readers, to engage not just with the words of Langri Thangpa's important work but, more importantly, with the intent and aims animating this short text.

# 5. Eight Verses on Mind Training (original)

## *Langri Thangpa*

1

With the wish to achieve the highest aim,
which surpasses even a wish-fulfilling gem,
I will train myself to at all times
cherish every sentient being as supreme.

2

Whenever I interact with others,
I will view myself as inferior to all,
and I will train myself
to hold others as superior from the depths of my heart.

3

In all my activities I will probe my mind,
and as soon as an affliction arises—
since it endangers myself and others—
I will train myself to confront it directly and avert it.

4

When I encounter beings of unpleasant character
and those oppressed by intense negative karma and
    suffering,
as though finding a treasure of precious jewels,
I will train myself to cherish them, for they are so rarely found.

5
When others out of jealousy
treat me wrongly with abuse and slander,
I will train to take upon myself the defeat
and offer to others the victory.

6
Even if someone I have helped
or in whom I have placed great hope
gravely mistreats me in hurtful ways,
I will train myself to view him as my sublime teacher.

7
In brief, I will train myself to offer benefit and joy
to all my mothers, both directly and indirectly,
and respectfully take upon myself
all the hurts and pains of my mothers.

8
By ensuring that all this remains unsullied
by the stains of the eight mundane concerns,
and by understanding all things as illusions,
I will train myself to be free of the bondage of clinging.

# Eight Verses on Mind Training (revised)

1
With the wish to achieve the highest aim,
which surpasses even a wish-fulfilling gem,
for the benefit of all sentient beings,
may I hold them dear at all times.

2
Whenever I interact with another,
may I view myself as the lowest among all
and, from the very depths of my heart,
hold others as superior.

3
In all my activities may I probe my mind,
and as soon as an affliction arises—
since it endangers myself and others—
may I confront it directly and avert it.

4
When I encounter beings of unpleasant character
and those oppressed by intense negativity and suffering,
as though finding a treasure of precious jewels,
may I cherish them, for they are so rarely found.

5
When others out of jealousy
treat me wrongly with abuse and slander,
may I take upon myself the defeat
and offer to others the victory.

6
Even if someone I have helped
or in whom I have placed great hope
gravely mistreats me in hurtful ways,
may I view him as my sublime teacher.

7
In brief, may I offer benefit and joy
to all my mothers, both directly and indirectly,
and may I quietly take upon myself
all the hurts and pains of my mothers.

8
May all of this remain unsullied
by the stains of the eight mundane concerns,
and, by understanding all things as illusions,
free of clinging, may I be released from bondage.

# 6. A Commentary on
## "Eight Verses on Mind Training"
### Chekawa Yeshé Dorjé

HEREIN IS *Eight Verses on Mind Training* together with the story of its origin.

I pay homage to the sublime teachers!

Geshe Chekawa once remarked, "My admiration for the Kadampas first arose when I heard the eight verses from Chakshingwa.[87] Thereafter I studied the verses and meticulously memorized the words, repeating them until I arrived at Lungshö Gegong, yet I failed to realize their meaning in my heart. For if these verses had entered my heart, things would have been quite different by then. Nonetheless, whenever the fear of being attacked [by bandits and such] appeared in my mind during my journey, I reflected upon these verses and this helped. Also I was often in situations where I had to seek shelter with strangers when my mind turned wild and untamed. During times when I was confronted with seemingly unbearable situations, such as failing to secure a suitable shelter, or when I became the target of others' disparagement, these verses helped me."

What verses are these? They are the following eight verses:

> With the wish to achieve the highest aim,
> which surpasses even a wish-fulfilling gem,

> **I will train myself to at all times
> cherish every sentient being as supreme.**

In general, in order to train yourself to view each sentient being as a wish-fulfilling gem, recall two similarities shared by sentient beings and the precious gem. First if you submerge the wish-fulfilling gem in a muddy mire, the gem cannot cleanse itself of the mud; however, if you wash it with scented water on a full-moon day, adorn the tip of a victory banner with it, and make offerings to it, the gem can then become a source of all earthly wishes. In the same way, sentient beings afflicted with the various defects of cyclic existence cannot free themselves from the mire of this unenlightened state, nor can they wash away their sufferings and the origins of these sufferings. However, with our help, all the benefits, both immediate and ultimate, can issue from them. Without sentient beings, how would you obtain even the immediate benefits—these would cease immediately; even ultimate happiness arises in relation to sentient beings. It is on the basis of sentient beings that you attain the unsurpassable state of buddhahood.

Second, in particular:

> **Whenever I interact with others,
> I will view myself as inferior to all,
> and I will train myself
> to hold others as superior from the depths of my heart.**

As stated here, wherever we are and whomever we interact with, we should train to view ourselves, in all possible ways, as lower and to respect others from the depths of our heart. "Others" encompasses those who are higher than us, such as our spiritual teachers; those who are equal to us, such as our fellow monks; and those who are inferior to us, such as beggars. "In all respects" refers to our family ancestry, cognitive ability, and similar factors. We should reflect upon our own shortcomings in relation to these factors and avoid becoming proud. Thinking, "They all belong to the lowly class of butchers," we tend to generate pride on the basis of our physical appearance and walk as if we possess a skin akin to the color of rusted gold. So we are not even worthy of a sentient being's gaze!

With respect to our cognitive abilities, if we feel proud despite our commonplace lack of distinction, reflect, "I am ignorant of every one of the five fields of knowledge. Even in those fields where I have listened with care and attention, I fail to discern when I miss certain words and their explanations. In my behavior, too, though I am known to be a monk, there are hardly any negative deeds I have not committed. Even at this very moment, my thoughts embody the three poisons, and my actions of body, speech, and mind remain mostly impure. Therefore, in the future, it will be difficult to attain birth in the higher realms, let alone liberation."

Śāntideva's *Guide to the Bodhisattva's Way of Life* states:

> By this type of behavior,
> even the human form will not be obtained;
> if I fail to achieve human existence,
> there is only evil and no virtue.[88]

In this manner we should contemplate all our shortcomings and reflect, "Nothing falls beneath me but this river," and diminish our conceit and learn to respect others. This suggests that whenever we perceive positive qualities in others, or perceive qualities pertaining to family ancestry, physical appearance, material resources, or spiritual realizations such as the six perfections, we should think, "How wondrous indeed that they possess these qualities despite their flawed natures!" If, instead, they lack these qualities, we should reflect, "Who knows what higher qualities they may actually possess?" Here the story of the ugly mendicant is told.[89]

"From the depths" or the very bone "of my heart" indicates that our thoughts should not remain in our mouth as mere words. Instead, if we have the intention "I will regard all beings as my family without discriminating on the basis of their family background," even the noble Avalokiteśvara will applaud us with the statement, "O child of noble family, this is excellent!" Just as, when the earth is leveled, oceans form upon it and draw forth the waters, the supramundane qualities flourish in the hearts of those free of pride. Therefore the *Condensed Perfection of Wisdom* states:

> Abide as if you were a servant of all beings.[90]

In essence, the three scriptural collections are a means to vanquish conceit. When we think we are exceptional, we are unable to live in harmony with others even in this present life. As for its detrimental consequences in the next life, it is said:

> Some ignorant ones, due to the force of their conceit,
> take birth in the lower realms and in places bereft of
>     leisure;
> they take birth as paupers or among the lowly castes;
> and they become blind, weak, or possessed of a vile
>     demeanor.

[Because of conceit] our tendency for afflictions will deepen, and we will generate intense afflictions relative to those we deem below us. There is even a consequence more serious than this: we will fail to attain enlightenment. For it is written:

The bodhisattva who is conceited
remains far away from enlightenment.[91]

So all the states of inferiority, degeneration, and suffering within the bounds of mundane existence arise from grasping at our own self as most precious. In contrast, all the joys—both mundane and supramundane—originate from sentient beings. We should therefore perceive all sentient beings as embodiments of higher qualities and vanquish our pride.

Third, since the afflictions impede us from proceeding in the above manner, eliminate them as follows:

> **In all my activities I will probe my mind,**
> **and as soon as an affliction arises—**
> **since it endangers myself and others—**
> **I will train myself to confront it directly and avert it.**

Training ourselves to examine our mental continuum in all our activities and averting the afflictions as soon as they arise is as follows: Whichever of the four everyday activities we engage in,[92] with mindfulness and vigilance, we should analyze whether thoughts such as attachment arise in our mind. With the thought "I will relinquish them the instant they arise," we should level them flat by observing them in this manner. Instead, if we act like an elderly couple being robbed by a thief, we procrastinate and then nothing happens. If afflictions proliferate in our mental continuum, emotions like anger will also increase exponentially. A sutra states:

> Likewise, those who place their faith in sleep
> will procrastinate and fall further into slumber.
> This is true also of those who are lustful
> and those who crave intoxicants.

Our tendency for afflictions will deepen, and we will experience intense afflictions toward all we deem below us. A more serious consequence is that we ourselves will experience acute suffering. If we relinquish the afflictions, their propensities too will become lighter. The past propensities will weaken, and only subtle propensities will be created anew toward desirable objects. Since the law of cause and effect is subtle, the effects will definitely be realized in our experience. So we should view the afflictions as our enemies and enhance the power of their antidotes.

Śāntideva states:

> I may be slain or burned alive;
> likewise I may be decapitated;
> under no circumstance will I
> bow before my enemy, the afflictions.[93]

As stated here, the conventional enemy can harm us only in this world and not beyond, but the enemy that is our afflictions can injure us throughout all our lives. As it is said:

> This enemy of mine, the afflictions,
> is long-lived, with neither beginning nor end;
> no other enemies can endure
> in this manner for so long.[94]

Furthermore, when we surrender to our conventional enemies, they no longer harm us and may actually benefit us. If we give in to the afflictions in the same manner, however, they become even more destructive. As it is said:

> If you relate to your enemies with friendship and gifts,
> these bring benefit and happiness.

However, if you appease the afflictions,
it brings ever more suffering and injury.[95]

Furthermore, conventional enemies harm only our body, life, and wealth, whereas the afflictions create immeasurable suffering in this cycle of existence. As it is said:

Even were all the gods and demigods
to rise up against me as my enemies,
they could not drag me and cast me
into the blazing fire of the eternal hells.

Yet this powerful enemy, my afflictions,
can fling me instantly
where even mighty Mount Meru
would be crushed to dust on contact.[96]

So view the afflictions as our enemy and discard them. While conventional enemies can return and cause harm even after they have been banished, the afflictions enemy cannot resurface once it has been eradicated. It is like burnt seeds. The method for eliminating them is through conduct, meditation, and view.[97]

For beginners, given the weakness of their antidotes and their difficulty in countering afflictions that have already arisen, they must relinquish them first through their conduct. As for meditation, it is said that each affliction has a corresponding antidote. Since whatever meditative practice we undertake from among the three scopes becomes a remedy against all the afflictions, it is appropriate to engage in this practice. As our mental level advances, since afflictions are devoid of objects, it is sufficient simply to recognize that this is so. Thus there remains nothing to eliminate. Śāntideva states:

Afflictions! Afflictions! Relinquish them with your eyes
of insight.[98]

Fourth, training ourselves to regard beings of unpleasant character and those oppressed by powerful negative karma and suffering with special care and as something rarely found is
presented in the following:

> When I encounter beings of unpleasant character
> and those oppressed by intense negative karma and
>    suffering,
> as though finding a treasure of precious jewels,
> I will train myself to cherish them, for they are so
>    rarely found.

"Beings of unpleasant character" refers to those like the king
Asaṅga,[99] who, not having accumulated merit in the past, experience the arising of afflictions without even a trace of control.
It also refers to beings such as the person who, while crossing a
mountain pass, was given a plate of meat stew: When the food
burned his lips, he tossed the full plate away along with the pan
and bellowed, "You dare burn me!" "Intense negative karma"
refers to the five heinous crimes, degeneration of the vows, and
misappropriation of offerings made to the Three Jewels.
"Those oppressed by intense . . . suffering" refers to those who
are afflicted by leprosy, other serious illnesses, and so on.

We should not treat them as our enemies, saying, "We cannot
even look at them, and we must never allow them to come near
us." Rather we should feel compassion toward them, as though
they were being led away by the king's executioners. Even if
some among them are morally degenerate, we should feel,
"What can I do to help them?" until our tears flow freely. This
means that we should first console them with words, and if this

proves ineffective, we should provide for their material needs and render help to cure their illness. If this, too, is unsuccessful, we should sustain them in our thoughts, and in action we should protect them even with shelter. Some people, thinking, "This will not benefit the other, but it could harm me," cover their noses and walk away from those oppressed by acute suffering. Even so, there is no certainty that such suffering will never befall us. Therefore, in our actions, we should provide others with food, medicine, and the like, while with our thoughts we should contemplate the following and train the mind:

> Whatever sufferings beings have,
> may they all ripen upon me.[100]

The line "I will train myself to cherish them, for they are so rarely found" is explained as follows. Since it is rare to find a precious gem, we do not discard it but rather keep it and cherish it. In the same way, beings of unpleasant character are not so easy to find; yet in dependence upon them compassion arises, and in dependence upon them the awakening mind arises. Without making deliberate efforts, it is rare to encounter such objects as these that allow us to develop the Mahayana paths. Why? Because the noble ones and those with worldly excellence do not arouse our compassion, so they cannot help us enhance the awakening mind. They cannot therefore lead us to the attainment of buddhahood. This is stated in the following:

> Except for the awakening mind,
> the buddhas do not uphold any means.[101]

Fifth, training ourselves to accept the defeat without resentment, even when faced with slander and other injustices, is presented in the following:

> **When others out of jealousy**
> **treat me wrongly with abuse and slander,**
> **I will train to take upon myself the defeat**
> **and offer to others the victory.**

Whether or not we are at fault, if others slander us or malign us out of jealousy or other motives, instead of harboring resentment, we should respond with a gentle mind. Free of resentment, we should refrain from claiming, for instance, "I am innocent. Others are to blame." Like Langri Thangpa, we should take the defeat upon ourselves. It is said that whenever misfortunes befell another, he would say, "I too am in him." When we engage in charity and ethical discipline at present, we do so to purify our negative karma and accumulate merit. If we recognize those who slander us as sources of kindness, although this is not a substitute for the aforementioned two activities, it nevertheless cleanses us of resentment and purifies our negative karma, the master said. Taking the defeat upon ourselves prevents us from adding to our negative karma.[102]

Langri Thangpa states, "When it comes to purifying negative karma and accumulating merit, it is more effective to recognize those who baselessly slander you as great sources of kindness than it is to offer buttery delicacies to every monk in Phenyül." *A Guide to the Bodhisattva's Way of Life* states:

> Since it is in dependence upon
> his malign intention that forbearance arises,
> it's really he who is the cause of forbearance;
> like the true Dharma, he is worthy of veneration.[103]

To substantiate this assertion, Śāntideva states in the following that forbearance is more powerful than ethical discipline:

There is no negativity like anger,
and there is no virtue like forbearance. . . .[104]

This presents the forbearance of being unperturbed by harms.[105]

Sixth is the forbearance of voluntarily accepting suffering. When someone to whom we have rendered help in the past, or in whom we have placed great hope, betrays or slanders us, we should contemplate him as our teacher with a sense of gratitude. This is presented in the following:

> **Even if someone I have helped**
> **or in whom I have placed great hope**
> **gravely mistreats me in hurtful ways,**
> **I will train myself to view him as my sublime teacher.**

As for expectation, Dromtönpa once remarked, "In Kham, I went to visit the teacher Sherap Bar, a spiritual friend close to my heart. I went knowing he had not invited me, and he took offense at this and sent me away from his presence. He ordered others to remove all my belongings, and had me locked in a dark room. That was when it became clear whether I had trained my mind in loving-kindness and compassion, and whether the lines 'May these sufferings ripen upon me, / and may all my happiness ripen upon them'[106] had remained a lie for me." So we must never retaliate with resentment.

Furthermore, relating this to our own situation, were it not for sordid karma, such events would not befall us. As it has been said:

> Previously I caused harms
> such as these to other sentient beings,
> so it is right that today such injuries befall me,
> I who have harmed others.[107]

We should think that we ourselves are to blame [for whatever befalls us]; and in this manner, by maintaining a warm heart, we remain happy. And because we do not transfer the blame to others, they too remain happy. We should reflect, "This is due to my own karma. It is established that no one harms the noble ones who have eliminated their negative karma." Even from the other's perspective, it is our own negative karma that caused them to injure us. Reflect, "Because of me, he will have to go to the lower realms. I am to blame for this." It has been said:

> Impelled by my own karma,
> others have brought this harm upon me;
> because of this they'll fall to the pits of hell.
> So is it not I who has destroyed them?[108]

Thus it is appropriate to protect these beings from their suffering. Again, it is said:

> Those who falsely accuse me,
> And others who cause me harm,
> Likewise those who insult me:
> May they all share in enlightenment.[109]

Also:

> Even if others return kindness with harm,
> I will practice responding with great compassion;
> the most excellent beings of this world
> answer injury with benevolence.[110]

"To view them as spiritual teachers while thinking of their great kindness" refers to the following: Our spiritual teachers are embodiments of great kindness, for they bestow on us the vows, provide us with the methods of meditative practice, and reveal to us the path to liberation. Of course, if we fail to contemplate this and fail to guard this contemplation, we will not tread the path. So reflect, "What this being has given me helps purify my negative karma and accomplish my accumulations. He has therefore benefited me. So I must view him as my spiritual teacher, no different from the one who has conferred on me the oral transmissions of the meditative practices." In this respect, *Songs of Bliss*[111] states:

> Whether someone is foe or friend—
> these objects that give rise to afflictions—
> he who sees them as spiritual teachers
> will be joyful wherever he resides.

When such thoughts arise spontaneously, our mind is trained; then, even if we have no other practice, whatever acts we engage in turn into the path to enlightenment. This is like the saying, "One cannot find excrement in a land of gold."

*Dharma* is the transformation of your mind and not the transformation of the external world. For a trained person, even if the three worlds—of humans, celestial gods, and demons— were to rise up as his enemies, his mind would not be afflicted by nonvirtue and suffering. Since no one can vanquish him, he is called a *hero*.

Seventh, in brief, one must train to offer—both directly and indirectly—all the benefits and joys to our dear mother sentient beings and to take all their hurts and pains into the depths of our hearts. This is presented in the following:

**In brief, I will train myself to offer benefit and joy**
**to all my mothers, both directly and indirectly,**

**and respectfully take upon myself**
**all the hurts and pains of my mothers.**

"In brief" refers to condensing all the preceding points. "Respectfully" suggests that we take these into the depths of our hearts while contemplating the kindness of our mothers. In other words, we should practice giving and taking not merely in words but from the depths of our hearts. In practice, if we give away such causes of well-being as food, medicine, and so on while taking upon ourselves all the hurts and pains of sentient beings, this is a cause for achieving birth in higher realms and attaining definitive goodness.[112] If, however, we are not yet able to actually practice this, we should instead perform the taking mentally by engaging in the meditation of giving and taking and dedicating all our joys of this life. When making aspiration prayers, we should utter from the depth of our hearts the following lines from *A Guide to the Bodhisattva's Way of Life*:

> My own happiness and others' suffering—
> If I do not thoroughly exchange them,
> I will not become fully enlightened;
> in this cyclic existence, too, I'll find no joy.[113]

Eighth, since in all these practices it is possible to become defiled, we should make sure that they remain untainted by even the slightest mundane consideration of this life, and with the awareness that recognizes all phenomena as illusion-like, we should train to be utterly free of attachment. This is presented in the following:

**By ensuring that all this remains unsullied**
**by the stains of the eight mundane concerns,**

**and by understanding all things as illusions,**
**I will train myself to be free of the bondage of clinging.**

Thus the remedy—the method—is this. When tainted with mundane concerns such as the desire to be perceived by others as praiseworthy, we fall under the influence of the eight mundane concerns, and our pursuits become those of self-interest. When this occurs, then the sacred teachings have been turned into demons. If we understand these mundane concerns as akin to illusions, later we will relinquish them. Nothing within our present experience possesses substantial reality.

> So among these empty phenomena,
> what is there to gain or to lose?
> Who provides you with what service?
> And who subjects you to insults?
>
> From whence do pleasure and pain arise?
> What is there to be sad or joyful about?[114]

And further,

> That all things are just like space,
> I, for one, shall accept.[115]

As for supplicating all [objects of refuge] and reciting this as an aspiration, it is as follows: We should make mandala offering to the teachers and the Three Jewels and make the following supplication:

"If you—my teachers, the buddhas of the three times, and all the bodhisattvas—possess blessings and compassion; if you—the ten male and ten female wrathful deities—possess power and might; and if you—the wisdom ḍākinīs—possess strength and abilities, bless me so that the meaning of these eight verses will be realized in me. Bless me so that all the suffering and causes of suffering of all sentient beings ripens upon me and that all the fruits of my awakening mind ripen upon all beings." We thus train by relating in this way to the four truths.[116]

Whatever virtuous actions, such as these mind training practices, we may perform, afterward we should recite this aspiration prayer of the eight verses. Making such an aspiration creates propensities for the awakening mind. We should recite the following aspiration prayer: "To such activities of root virtue I will dedicate all my time—all my months and all my years. In the future, too, I will make sure to encounter spiritual teachers and to associate with virtuous companions." We should recite these prayers of aspiration regularly.

This commentary on the eight verses of the bodhisattva Langri Thangpa was composed by Chekawa Yeshé Dorjé. This commentary on the root verses constitutes a profound instruction on mind training. Please strive in this. May its realization arise in the hearts of all.

# Equanimity

In most Tibetan sources, including *Mind Training: The Great Collection*, the short text *Leveling Out All Conceptions* is attributed to Serlingpa, the teacher from whom Atiśa is said to have received the instructions on mind training on the Indonesian island of Sumatra. It is difficult to determine how far to accept this traditional Tibetan attribution. In the colophon at the end of commentary, this attribution appears to have come from an account given by Master Atiśa. The text itself has a decidedly authoritative voice, and its literary style suggests a certain antiquity. Interestingly, if the attribution to Serlingpa is correct, it suggests that this teaching was given at the behest of Atiśa as he was planning his journey to Tibet, and the expression "barbarian borderlands" it mentions was probably meant to allude to Tibet.

As its title suggests, the central theme of this short text seems to be challenging our habitual thought patterns and their underlying assumptions. The work opens with what might be understood as the four principal objectives of a spiritual practitioner: (1) leveling out all conceptions, (2) engaging the forces of all the antidotes, (3) concentrating all aspirations into a single point, and (4) seeking the path where all paths converge. A key injunction in leveling out all conceptions is to engage the antidote the moment a conception arises. As made clear in the commentary, this means we do not allow ourselves to be swept away by the undertow of habitual thought processes. We are admonished instead, in stanzas 3–4, to respond to thoughts decisively through applying four antidotes, or recognitions: that all adversities are spiritual teachers, that nonhuman agents of harm are emanations of the buddhas, that sickness is a broom that clears away negative karma and defilements, and finally, that sufferings are displays of the *dharmadhātu*, the expanse of ultimate reality. In these instructions, we find unmistakable expressions of the classic mind training injunction to transform adversities into the path of enlightenment.

Stanzas 5–6 instruct us to move beyond transforming adversities to a more radical practice where we deliberately invite in what we normally take to be intensely adverse conditions. Mind training here counteracts pleasure, which, when not offset, often leads to excessive attachment. It is also a "successor to misery" in that you use mind training to deliberately aggravate your suffering to gain greater benefit from it. In addition, mind training can be like a charm that attracts additional misfortune to fuel your practice. Finally, mind training is like a single genuinely meaningful wish that puts a lid on all the myriad utterly meaningless ones we generate.

In stanzas 7–8, we are then exposed to the heart of *lojong*, radically transforming our habitual self-centeredness to a compassionate, other-centered stance, both in our basic attitude and in our actions. Although the commentary explicitly mentions only the taking of others' suffering, which is the "taking" aspect of *tonglen* (giving and taking), that it is *tonglen* practice that is being referred to here is quite clear.

Finally, stanzas 9–10 present the instruction on how to bring the understanding of emptiness, the ultimate nature of reality, into our practice. Speaking in terms of what it calls the "four aspects of the sealing of emptiness"—(1) casting away decisively all conceptions rooted in subject-object duality, (2) letting go of all conceptions with ease within the sphere free of conceptual elaborations, (3) dismantling thoroughly the temporal sequence of thoughts so that they do not form a causal chain, and (4) letting our mind rest in its natural state without any reification or denigration—the text presents a succinct and unique way to sever our attachment to habitual thoughts and perceptions. Although the commentary does not state this, the final section of this text has unmistakable resonance with the teachings of the *dohā* songs of realization, especially those of the Indian adept Saraha, which Atiśa clearly knew. Both the mind training texts and the *dohā* teachings emphasize eliminating all forms of conceptualization.

Thus stanzas 7–10 presents what is, in the language of the *Seven-Point*, the "main practice" of cultivating the two awakening minds—conventional awakening mind, which is the altruistic aspiration to achieve buddhahood for the benefit of all beings, and ultimate awakening mind, the direct realization of emptiness.

*Mind Training: The Great Collection* contains an interesting if somewhat mythologized account of Atiśa's long sea voyage to Sumatra to meet with Master Serlingpa. Apart from this account, few texts provide any clear depiction of Serlingpa. That he was a Buddhist scholar of great stature in the tenth and eleventh centuries remains beyond doubt,[117] but most of what we know of the life of Serlingpa, whose personal name is Dharmakīrti, comes largely from the biographies of Atiśa composed by Tibetan authors.

For example, the "standard biography" of Atiśa by Chim Namkha Drak (1210–85) provides such details as his premonastic name, his arousal of faith in the Dharma as a result of coming face to face with a statue of the Buddha, his subsequent visit to Bodhgaya, the name of his Indian teacher, and so on. Given the specific nature of these details, it appears that Chim had access to some earlier source, most possibly Naktso

Lotsāwa's *Great Narrative*, which is no longer extant. Naktso spent many years with Atiśa, often serving him as the Tibetan half of a translation team, so the accounts related to Atiśa's teachers could easily have come from Master Atiśa himself. Indeed many of the six texts attributed to Serlingpa in the Tibetan canon were translated by the team of Atiśa and Naktso.

So, regardless of how much of the narrative of Atiśa's voyage to Sumatra and his subsequent tutelage under Serlingpa in the later biographies is true, there is little doubt that Serlingpa's teaching on the awakening mind forms the core of Atiśa's mind training instructions.

# 7. Leveling Out All Conceptions
*Attributed to Serlingpa*

THE GUARDIAN and teacher Serlingpa said to Master Atiśa, "Son, to subdue the barbarian borderlands, you will need the following teachings:"[118]

1
Level out all [false] conceptions,
carry forth the force of all antidotes,
concentrate all aspirations into one,
and seek the path where all paths converge.

2
These are the four enlightened factors, the antidotes.
They are vital if you are to tame barbarian borderlands,
and they are essential, too, in the age of degeneration,
to bear up amid the misguided ways of negative companions.

3
Adverse conditions are your spiritual teacher,
demons and possessor spirits, the Buddha's emanations;
sickness is a broom for negative karma and defilements,
and sufferings are displays of the *dharmadhātu*, ultimate
   reality's expanse.

4

These are the four thoroughly afflicted factors.
They are vital if you are to tame the barbarian
    borderlands,
and they are essential, too, in the era of degeneration,
to bear up amid the misguided ways of negative
    companions.


5

This training is the great counterbalance to happiness,
and the great successor to misery;
it is a charm that attracts misfortune,
and a wish capping the useless ones.[119]


6

These are the four antidotes to misguided ways.
They are vital if you are to tame the barbarian borderlands,
and they are essential, too, in the age of degeneration,
to bear up amid the misguided ways of negative
    companions.


7

"Self" is the root of negative karma;
it is to be discarded decisively.
"Other" is a source of enlightenment;
it is to be embraced enthusiastically.


8

These two teachings draw the remedies to a close;
they are vital if you are to tame the barbarian borderlands,
and they are essential, too, in the age of degeneration,
to bear up amid the misguided ways of negative companions.

9
Cast away decisively, let go with ease,
dismantle thoroughly, and let be with gentleness:
These are the four aspects of the sealing of emptiness.[120]
They are vital if you are to tame the barbarian borderlands.

10
They are essential, too, in the age of degeneration,
to bear up amid the misguided ways of negative companions.
If you engage in the practices in this way,
beings will not be fettered but will attain freedom.

Thus it was taught.

# 8. A Commentary on "Leveling Out All Conceptions"[121]

## Attributed to Atisa

WITH GREAT REVERENCE I pay homage to and seek refuge in the precious teacher Lord Serlingpa and his entire lineage, father and sons. Pray bless me!

Lord Serlingpa, the embodiment of wisdom and great compassion, once said to Atisa, "My son, in order to serve others during this era of degeneration, you must distill the sacred words of the discourses, scriptures, and reasonings, and all the pith instructions of the teachers and undertake their practice in one sitting. For this you will require the following teaching, which makes you invulnerable to sickness, harm, interference from obstructive forces, demons, and upholders of false teachings, and all such adverse conditions and impediments." Then he taught the following:

> Level out all [false] conceptions,
> carry forth the force of all antidotes,
> concentrate all aspirations into one,
> and seek the path where all paths converge.
>
> These are the four enlightened factors, the antidotes.
> They are vital if you are to tame barbarian borderlands,
> and they are essential, too, in the age of degeneration,
> to bear up amid the misguided ways of negative companions.

The meaning of these verses is as follows. It is essential that you level out the conceptions at the very site of their origin. Examine, "Where do these appear? To what sense faculties do they appear? In what shape and color do they appear?" They are like a venomous snake or a rabid dog; do not allow them to be near you. Rather, without giving in to procrastination, destroy them the moment they arise by applying their antidote. It has been stated in a sutra:

> O attachment, I've now discerned your root:
> You arise from the proliferation of concepts.[122]

Also:

> Conceptualization is the great ignorance
> that casts one into samsara's ocean.[123]

*Entering the Middle Way* states:

> Ordinary beings are chained by their conceptualization;
> yogis who are free of conceptualization gain freedom.
> That which reveals the falsity of conceptualizations,
> the learned ones taught, is the fruit of a thorough
> analysis.[124]

All the sacred scriptures and the treatises of the Great Vehicle, such as those cited here, assert conceptualization to be a great obstacle to attaining enlightenment. It is crucial, therefore, not to delay. Since, as it says here, harboring too many thoughts prevents you from going very far, do not engage in the proliferation of thoughts, even with respect to the profound truth. Rather, consolidate your aspirations decisively on the single task of destroying [false] conceptions. Even the sutras describe mental engagements as Māra's activity.

Therefore, until you attain omniscient buddhahood, concentrate all your aspirations and relate all the grounds and paths—such as the paths of accumulation, seeing, and meditation—to destroying false conceptions the instant they arise by applying their antidotes. In brief, every time a conceptualization arises, make sure that its antidote arrives there too. For it is through antidotes that your aspirations must be concentrated to destroy false conceptions; and all the paths, too, must be traversed by way of destroying these false conceptions. For this purpose, adopt the four factors belonging to the class of enlightened phenomena.[125]

Again, the following was taught:

> Adverse conditions are your spiritual teacher,
> demons and possessor spirits, the Buddha's emanations;
> sickness is a broom for negative karma and defilements,
> and sufferings are displays of the *dharmadhātu*,
>     ultimate reality's expanse.
>
> These are the four thoroughly afflicted factors.
> They are vital if you are to tame the barbarian borderlands,
> and they are essential, too, in the era of degeneration,
> to bear up amid the misguided ways of negative
>     companions.

The meaning of these lines is as follows: Even if unwanted adverse conditions such as sickness and suffering befall you, turn these into catalysts and take on top of these the sickness and suffering of all sentient beings. Take these on mentally, without reservation, and rejoice for having taken them en masse. Similarly, as you give to sentient beings whatever favorable conditions you enjoy, such as your happiness, rejoice in sentient beings perfecting their accumulations of merit. Likewise, if you probe any conditions for the sights, sounds, smells, tastes, and so on that arise, they are nowhere to be found. Place your mind in this truth of unfindability, and rejoice in [adverse conditions with the thought], "They are my spiritual teachers exhorting me to the ultimate expanse; they are conditions conducive to enlightenment."

When harms from ghosts, ogresses, site spirits, and so on befall you, place upon these, with your entire heart, whatever harms and sufferings sentient beings are undergoing. Thinking "I have definitely taken these," cultivate a sense of joy. By giving to the agents of harm whatever they desire—such as the flesh, blood, and so on of your body—out of compassion, out of loving-kindness, and out of the awakening mind, the harms are turned into factors conducive to attaining enlightenment and therefore assist your journey to enlightenment. Given that all these malevolent forces are emanations of the buddhas, you should cultivate inconceivable joy and respect toward them.

When you are suffering from an illness, take all the sickness and pains of sentient beings into the very core of your heart and imagine that all sentient beings attain perfect abandonment. Thinking, "This has served its purpose," cultivate joy. When you are free of sickness, again motivated thus, give to sentient beings all your happiness and its causes and imagine that all sentient beings attain perfect realization. Thinking, "This has served its purpose," cultivate joy. This sweeps away negative karma and the obscurations, for it does not allow negative karma and obscurations to linger unchallenged for even a single moment. If a hundred sufferings arise, a hundred ways to search for [their true nature] will emerge. However, given that these [sufferings] never truly existed, there are a hundred different ways to not find them. These are therefore the hundred abandonments and the hundred realizations—a great display of the ultimate expanse. Cultivate joy in this. These, then, are the objects to be relinquished, the four thoroughly unenlightened factors.

Again, the following was taught:

> This training is the great counterbalance to happiness,
> and the great successor to misery;
> it is a charm that attracts misfortune,
> and a wish capping the useless ones.[126]
>
> These are the four antidotes to misguided ways.
> They are vital if you are to tame the barbarian borderlands,
> and they are essential, too, in the age of degeneration,
> to bear up amid the misguided ways of negative
>   companions.

The meaning of these lines is as follows: Harbor modest desires and cultivate contentment to counteract the longing for pleasures such as food, drink, wealth, fame, and so on, for these obstruct the pursuit of virtuous activities. Similarly, follow up sufferings with additional pain: If your leg hurts, go for circumambulation; if your back hurts, do prostrations; if you suffer too much greed, give things away to others; if you suffer distractions, enter into retreat; and if you delight in gossip, cease speaking. When you suffer great unwanted omens—such as a bad reputation, disputes, magical spells, and malicious gossip—since these are means for subduing the malevolent demon of self-grasping, welcome them as auspicious. As you might use a charm to attract good fortune, cultivate courage by shouting, "Send me more!" With the thought, "All these events befalling me, events that are normally of no benefit, if I can use them to subdue this self, from here on I will not be reborn in cyclic existence." In this manner, you cap your desires and ensure that you achieve the strength of the three aspects of forbearance.[127]

These are, then, the four antidotes to misguided ways, the objects of thorough application of the antidotes.

Again, the following was taught:

> "Self" is the root of negative karma;
> it is to be discarded decisively.
> "Other" is a source of enlightenment;
> it is to be embraced enthusiastically.
>
> These two teachings draw the remedies to a close;
> they are vital if you are to tame the barbarian borderlands,
> and they are essential, too, in the age of degeneration,
> to bear up amid the misguided ways of negative companions.

The meaning of these lines is as follows: Given that the self is the source of all unwanted events and the root of all negative actions, you should never cherish it but discard it decisively. Reflect, "O enemies, if you like it, take it. O demons, if you like it, take it. If not in haste, cook it first; if in haste, just take it and run." In this way, totally discard your own self and serve the well-being of all. And since the joyful embracing of others' welfare through forsaking your own self-interest is the source of unsurpassable goodness, nurture sentient beings with kindness and take their sufferings upon yourself. These two teachings, which bring closure to the objects to be relinquished and their remedies, are the practice of great beings.

> Cast away decisively, let go with ease,
> dismantle thoroughly, and let be with gentleness:
> These are the four aspects of the sealing of emptiness.[128]
> They are vital if you are to tame the barbarian borderlands.

> They are essential, too, in the age of degeneration,
> to bear up amid the misguided ways of negative
>   companions.
> If you engage in the practices in this way,
> beings will not be fettered but will attain freedom.

The meaning of these lines is as follows: You should decisively cast away all dualistic thoughts of perceived objects and perceiving cognition and let your mind rest free and radiant, absent of conceptualization and bondage in the ultimate expanse that is free of conceptual elaboration. Do not chase after earlier instants of cognition; do not anticipate the future; but, free of clinging, let the present remain as it is. Let it rest free in its natural state, uncontrived and free of any exaggeration or denigration. These are the four aspects of the sealing of emptiness. If you practice in this manner, you will not be chained by karma in cyclic existence; rather you will be free and you will attain liberation.

Some practice other than this would fail to tame the barbarous sentient beings of this era of degeneration. Yet, possessing this, you will be immune to obstacles, and you will achieve the well-being of sentient beings with ease. Thus it was taught. I have here presented the teachings of the peerless Serlingpa in precise accordance with his words.[129]

\* \* \*

The *Amoghapāśa Tantra* states:

> "Wisdom" refers to enlightenment, while "hero" indicates skillful means; with these two, the welfare of sentient beings will be achieved.[130]

Again, the Guhyasamāja tantra entitled *Drop of Freedom* states:

> With compassion as the sole basis,
> all enlightened qualities will arise.[131]

Again:

> If the root of compassion is absent,
> one cannot endure hardships.[132]

The sutra entitled *Perfectly Gathering the Qualities* states:

> Whosoever aspires to attain full enlightenment
> swiftly should not train in many practices. What is
> that sole practice? It is great compassion. For
> whosoever possesses great compassion possesses in
> his palms all the teachings of the Buddha. He will
> achieve these without effort and without exertion.
> In brief, great compassion is the root of all the
> teachings.[133]

This instruction was given to Atiśa, the savior of beings, by
his teacher Serlingpa Dharmakīrti to help tame the barbarian
borderlands.

# KARMIC JUSTICE

AMONG ALL THE TEXTS in this volume, one of the most intriguing, in style as well as origin, is *Wheel of Sharp Weapons*.[134] With 116 verses, the work is composed in a lively poetic style in the form of self-recriminations as well as self-exhortation. Starting from its opening line, the verses focus on one of the paradigmatic themes of mind training—transforming adversities into the path to enlightenment. In addition, we hear unmistakable echoes of *tonglen*, taking on others' suffering and mental afflictions and offering to them our happiness and positive mental states, as well as the need to view others as a source of our own ultimate well-being, and the need to engage in all stages of the path with the awareness that all things are ultimately empty in nature. All of these are powerfully articulated in this work.

As its title suggests, the key metaphor used throughout is a wheel of sharp weapons. This traditional Indian weapon wheel has sharp double-edged knives extending outward from a central ring, which is spun like a frisbee at its target. In traditional Indian mythology, some gods carry this wheel as their weapon of choice, and the paintings of these gods depict the wheel hovering above their right index finger. This weapon is thought to have a kind of magic power that permits it to return to the owner, like a boomerang.

Clearly, the sentiments expressed in this poem will have

powerful resonance if the reader accepts the twin doctrines of karma and rebirth. However, even for readers who do not share these premises, these verses can evoke powerful insights and emotive response. For negative karmic deeds remain so regardless of our belief in the law of karma—even a purely secular standpoint recognizes that these acts bring suffering both to self and others. And the antidotes that are called for remain the same, too, again irrespective of our metaphysical perspective.

Since our volume does not contain a commentary to this text, I will provide a brief outline of its structure. In doing so, I am relying on the topical outline found in the collected works of the nineteenth-century Mongolian scholar Losang Tamdrin, who suggests that this topical outline may have been composed by the famed Geluk master Gungthang Tenpai Drönmé (1762–1823). Tamdrin notes that the version of the outline he found suffered from a substantial number of corruptions, all of which he corrected.

According to this topical outline, the text has three broad parts: (I) stanzas pertaining to the conventional awakening mind, that is, the altruistic aspiration to seek full awakening for the benefit of all beings (verses 1–102), (II) those pertaining to the ultimate awakening mind, that is, the direct realization of emptiness (103–15), and finally, (III) a verse for dedicating the merits of the practice. The verses can be further broken down as follows:

- How, in the forests of cyclic existence, the peacock-like heroic bodhisattvas transform self-grasping and mental afflictions into life-sustaining vital essences. (1–7)
- Practicing *tonglen*, giving one's happiness to others and taking others' suffering and its causes upon onself. (8)
- Correlating specific karma and their effects with their corresponding antidotes. (9–47)
- Recognizing the real enemy. (48)

- Supplicating the meditation deity Yamāntaka to help crush the demon of self-grasping through a rite of subjugation. (49–89)
- The heart of the supplication to Yamāntaka. (90–94)
- Dedication and aspiration prayers. (95–101)
- How, ultimately, the results of practice are attained. (102)
- Introducing all appearances to be empty of substantial reality. (103–13)
- Introducing the mind, too, to be empty of substantial reality. (114)
- Introducing the indivisibility of the appearances and mind. (115)
- Dedicating the merits. (116)

The section on supplicating Yamāntaka opens with the following powerful stanzas:

> Now, O Yamāntaka, raise the weapon of karma over
>   [the enemy's] head;
> spin the wheel three times fiercely over his head.
> Your legs of two truths stand apart and eyes of method
>   and wisdom wide open,
> with your fangs of four powers bared, strike the enemy!
>
> The king of spells who confounds the enemy's mind:
> summon this oath breaker who betrays self and others—
> this savage called "self-grasping demon,"
> who while brandishing the weapon of karma,
> runs amok in the jungle of cyclic existence.
>
> Summon him, summon him, wrathful Yamāntaka!
> Strike him, strike him, pierce the heart of this enemy,
>   the self!

> Dance and trample on the head of this betrayer, false
> conception!
> Mortally strike at the heart of this butcher and enemy,
> Ego!

The imagery here is quite striking. What we have is the personification of our habitual self-grasping and self-centeredness in the form of a demon, which is then being exorcised through invoking the power of Yamāntaka. Using the weapon wheel the deity is asked to crush the demonic ego, the oath-breaker, the savage "self-grasping demon," and then dance in celebration by trampling upon its head! To this day, when I find myself beginning to get caught in a spiral of thought that has the potential to lead to obsessive rumination, I chant to myself the line, "Dance and trample on the head of this betrayer, false conception!" Admittedly radical, I find this approach highly effective, for it immediately stops the racing thought process in its tracks.

I first came across these powerful lines as a young monk at Ganden by listening to a beautiful recording of this text by Kyabjé Trijang Rinpoché, the late junior tutor of His Holiness the Dalai Lama. Hearing the lines chanted in his deep melodious voice, I was entranced and immediately went out to look for the text. Later, I was able to receive instructions on the text both from my own teacher, Kyabjé Zemé Rinpoché, as well as once from His Holiness the Dalai Lama.

Traditional Tibetan sources attribute this text to one Dharmarakṣita, who is recognized as one of the "three Indian teachers" of Atiśa on mind training. We know very little in the way of personal details about this master, other than that he is supposed to have held a non-Mahayana philosophical standpoint and that he was a person of such great compassion that he once gave away a piece of his own flesh to help cure someone of an illness. We have no independent corroboration of the historicity of this person, but we do find mentions of him in very early sources, such as those of Dromtönpa. Thus it seems that Atiśa himself may have been the source of these details about Dharmarakṣita.

The provenance of the text itself is another question. We have no viable alternative to the traditional ascription, and the colophon states that the work was translated from Sanskrit by Atiśa and Dromtönpa. This said, I can find no explicit mention of this work in a text undisputedly dated prior to the late fourteenth or early fifteenth century. Several years ago, a large stash of texts associated with the Kadam school, the lineage founded by Dromtönpa, was found. As these texts are cataloged, we may find references to this *Wheel of Sharp Weapons* in an earlier source. As of now, however, its true origin is in question.

This text appeared to have become quite popular in the Geluk school around the early eighteenth century, with such luminaries as the Seventh Dalai Lama, Yongzin Yeshé Gyaltsen, Phurbuchok Ngawang Jampa, Gungthang Tenpai Drönmé, and Trichen Tenpa Rapgyé teaching it widely.

# 9. Wheel of Sharp Weapons

*Attributed to Dharmarakṣita*[135]

Homage to the Three Jewels!

THIS IS THE WHEEL of weapons striking at the vital points of the enemy's body.
Homage to the wrathful Yamāntaka![136]

1
When peacocks roam through the jungle of virulent poison,
though the gardens of medicinal plants may be attractive,
the peacock flocks will not indulge in them;
for peacocks thrive on the essence of virulent poison.

2
Likewise when heroic bodhisattvas enter the jungle of cyclic
    existence,
though the gardens of happiness and prosperity may seem
    beautiful,
the heroes will not become attached to them;
for heroes thrive in the forest of suffering.

3
Those who avidly pursue happiness and prosperity
are brought to suffering due to their cowardice.

Bodhisattvas, who willingly embrace suffering,
always remain happy due to their heroism.

4
Now here, desire is like the jungle of virulent poison;
the peacock-like heroes can digest this,
but for the crow-like cowards it spells death,
for how can the self-centered digest such poison?
When you extend this [analogy] to other afflictions,
each similarly assails liberation's life force, as [poison does]
    a crow.

5
Therefore peacock-like heroes must convert
afflictions, which resemble a jungle of poisons, into an elixir
and enter the jungle of cyclic existence;
embracing the afflictions, heroes must destroy their poison.

6
From now on I will distance myself from this demon's
    emissary—
self-grasping—which makes me wander helplessly
and seeks only selfish happiness and prosperity;
I will joyfully embrace hardship for the sake of others.

7
Propelled by karma and habituated to the afflictions:
I will heap upon this self that yearns for happiness
the sufferings of all beings who share this nature.

8
When selfish craving enters my heart,
I will expel it and offer my happiness to all beings.

If those around me rise in mutiny against me,
I will relish it, thinking, "This is due to my own negligence."

9
When my body falls prey to unbearable illnesses,
it is the weapon of evil karma returning on me
for injuring the bodies of others;
from now on I will take all sickness upon myself.

10
When my mind falls prey to suffering,
it is the weapon of evil karma turning upon me
for definitely causing turbulence in the hearts of others;
from now on I will take all suffering upon myself.

11
When I am tormented by extreme hunger and thirst,
it is the weapon of evil karma turning upon me
for engaging in deception, theft, and miserly acts;
from now on I will take all hunger and thirst upon myself.

12
When I am powerless and suffer in servitude to others,
it is the weapon of evil karma turning upon me
for being hostile to the weak and subjugating them;
from now on I will employ my body and life in the service of
    others.

13
When unpleasant words reach my ears,
it is the weapon of evil karma turning upon me
for my verbal offenses, such as divisive speech;
from now on I will condemn flawed speech.

14

When I am born in a place of impurity,
it is the weapon of evil karma turning upon me
for always cultivating impure perceptions;
from now on I will cultivate only pure perceptions.

15

When I become separated from helpful and loving friends,
it is the weapon of evil karma turning upon me
for luring away others' companions;
from now on I will never estrange others from their
     companions.

16

When the sublime ones become displeased with me,
it is the weapon of evil karma turning upon me
for renouncing the sublime ones and seeking bad companions;
from now on I will renounce negative friendships.

17

When others assail me with exaggeration, denigration,
     and so on,
it is the weapon of evil karma turning upon me
for disparaging sublime beings;
from now on I will never belittle others with disparaging
     words.

18

When my material resources waste away,
it is the weapon of evil karma turning upon me
for not respecting others' resources;
from now on I will help others find what they need.

19

When my mind becomes dull and my heart unhappy,
it is the weapon of evil karma turning upon me
for making others accumulate negative karma;
from now on I will shun enabling others' negative acts.

20

When I fail in my endeavors and feel deeply disturbed,
it is the weapon of evil karma turning upon me
for obstructing the work of sublime ones;
from now on I will relinquish all obstructive deeds.

21

When my gurus remain displeased no matter what I do,
it is the weapon of evil karma turning upon me
for acting duplicitously toward the sublime Dharma;
from now on I will be less duplicitous with respect to
   the Dharma.

22

When everyone challenges what I say,
it is the weapon of evil karma turning upon me
for disregarding shame and my conscience;
from now on I will refrain from troubling behavior.

23

When disputes arise as soon as my companions gather,
it is the weapon of evil karma turning upon me
for peddling my destructive, evil character in all
   directions;
from now on I will maintain good character wherever I am.

24

When all who are close to me rise up as enemies,
it is the weapon of evil karma turning upon me
for harboring harmful, evil intentions within;
from now on I will diminish deceit and guile.

25

When I am sick with a chronic ulcer or edema,
it is the weapon of evil karma turning upon me
for wrongfully and heedlessly using others' possessions;
from now on I will renounce acts such as plundering others'
    possessions.

26

When my body is struck suddenly by contagious disease,
it is the weapon of evil karma turning upon me
for committing acts that undermined my solemn pledges;
from now on I will renounce nonvirtue.

27

When my intellect becomes ignorant of all fields of
    knowledge,
it is the weapon of evil karma turning upon me
for persisting in activities that must be cast aside;
from now on I will cultivate the insights of learning
    and so on.[137]

28

When I am overwhelmed by sloth while practicing Dharma,
it is the weapon of evil karma turning upon me
for amassing obscurations to the sublime Dharma;
from now on I will undergo hardships for the sake of
    the Dharma.

29
When I delight in afflictions and am greatly distracted,
it is the weapon of evil karma turning upon me
for not contemplating impermanence and the defects of
   cyclic existence;
from now on I will increase my dissatisfaction with cyclic
   existence.

30
When I continue to regress despite all my efforts,
it is the weapon of evil karma turning upon me
for defying karma and the law of cause and effect;
from now on I will strive to accumulate merit.

31
When all the religious rituals I perform go amiss,
it is the weapon of evil karma turning upon me
for investing hope and expectation in forces of darkness;
from now on I will turn away from forces of darkness.

32
When my prayers to the Three Jewels are impotent,
it is the weapon of evil karma turning upon me
for not entrusting myself to the Buddha's way;
from now on I will rely solely on the Three Jewels.

33
When my imagination arises as veils and possessor spirits,
it is the weapon of evil karma turning upon me
for accumulating negative karma in relation to deities and
   their mantras;
from now on I will vanquish all negative conceptions.

34

When I am lost and wander like a powerless man,
it is the weapon of evil karma turning upon me
for driving others, such as my guru, away from their abodes;
from now on I will expel no one from his home.


35

When calamities such as frost and hailstorms occur,
it is the weapon of evil karma turning upon me
for failing to properly observe my pledges and moral precepts;
from now on I will keep my pledges pure.


36

When I am greedy but have no wealth,
it is the weapon of evil karma turning upon me
for failing to give charity and make offerings to the Three
    Jewels;
from now on I will strive in giving and offering.


37

When I am ugly and am mistreated by my companions,
it is the weapon of evil karma turning upon me
for crafting ugly images while seething with anger;
from now on I will be patient when creating the images
    of gods.


38

When attachment and anger erupt no matter what I do,
it is the weapon of evil karma turning upon me
for allowing my untamed evil mind to become rigid;
from now on I will root out this obstinate heart.

39

When all my meditative practices fail in their aims,
it is the weapon of evil karma turning on me
for allowing pernicious views to enter my heart;
from now on whatever I do will be solely for others' sake.

40

When my mind remains untamed despite spiritual practice,
it is the weapon of evil karma turning upon me
for eagerly pursuing mundane ambitions;
from now on I will concentrate on aspiring for liberation.

41

When I feel remorse as soon as I sit down and reflect,
it is the weapon of evil karma turning upon me
for being shamelessly fickle and clamoring for high status;
from now on I will be vigilant in my associations with
    others.

42

When I am deceived by others' treachery,
it is the weapon of evil karma turning upon me
for being vain and selfishly greedy;
from now on I will be discreet with respect to everything.

43

When my studies and teaching fall prey to attachment
    and anger,
it is the weapon of evil karma turning upon me
for failing to reflect on the ills of demons in my heart;
from now on I will examine adverse forces and over-
    come them.

44
When all the good I have done turns out badly,
it is the weapon of evil karma turning upon me
for repaying others' kindness with ingratitude;
from now on I will respectfully repay others' kindness.

45
In brief, when calamities strike me like bolts of lightning,
it is the weapon of evil karma turning upon me,
just like the ironsmith slain by his own sword;
from now on I will be heedful against negative acts.

46
When I undergo sufferings in the lower realms,
it is the weapon of evil karma turning upon me,
like an archer slain by his own arrow;
from now on I will be heedful against negative acts.

47
When the sufferings of the householder befall me,
it is the weapon of evil karma turning upon me,
like parents slain by their own cherished children;
from now I will rightly renounce worldly life.

48
Since that's the way things are, I've seized the enemy!
I've caught the thief who steals and deceives with stealth.
Aha! There is no doubt that it's this self-grasping indeed;
this charlatan deceives me by impersonating me.

49
Now, O Yamāntaka, raise the weapon of karma over his head;
spin the wheel three times fiercely over his head.

Your legs of two truths stand apart and eyes of method
  and wisdom wide open,
with your fangs of four powers bared, strike the enemy!

50
The king of spells who confounds the enemy's mind;
summon this oath breaker who betrays self and others—
this savage called "self-grasping demon,"
who while brandishing the weapon of karma,
runs amok in the jungle of cyclic existence.

51
Summon him, summon him, wrathful Yamāntaka!
Strike him, strike him, pierce the heart of this enemy, the self!
Dance and trample on the head of this betrayer, false
  conception!
Mortally strike at the heart of this butcher and enemy, Ego!

52
*Hūṃ! Hūṃ!* Great deity, display your miraculous powers!
*Dza! Dza!* Bind this enemy tightly!
*Phat! Phat!* Release us from all bondage!
*Shik! Shik!* I beseech you to cut the knot of grasping!

53
Appear before me, O Yamāntaka, my meditation deity!
Tear it! Tear it! Rip to shreds this very instant—
the leather sack of karma and the five poisonous afflictions
that mires me in karma's samsaric mud.

54
Even though he leads me to misery in the three lower realms,
I do not learn to fear him but rush to his source.

Dance and trample on the head of this betrayer, false conception!
Mortally strike at the heart of this butcher and enemy, Ego!

55

Though my desire for comfort is great, I do not gather its
    causes;
though I have little tolerance for pain, I am rife with the dark
    craving of greed.
Dance and trample on the head of this betrayer, false conception!
Mortally strike at the heart of this butcher and enemy, Ego!

56

Though I want immediate results, my efforts to achieve them
    are feeble;
though I pursue many tasks, I never complete a single one.
Dance and trample on the head of this betrayer, false conception!
Mortally strike at the heart of this butcher and enemy, Ego!

57

Though I am eager to make new friends, my loyalty and
    friendship are short-lived;
though I aspire for resources, I seek them through theft and
    extortion.[138]
Dance and trample on the head of this betrayer, false conception!
Mortally strike at the heart of this butcher and enemy, Ego!

58

Though skilled at flattery and innuendo, my discontent
    runs deep;
though diligently amassing wealth, I am chained by
    miserliness.
Dance and trample on the head of this betrayer, false conception!
Mortally strike at the heart of this butcher and enemy, Ego!

59

Though rarely rendering help to others, I remain most boastful;
though unwilling to take risks, I am bloated with ambition.
Dance and trample on the head of this betrayer, false conception!
Mortally strike at the heart of this butcher and enemy, Ego!

60

Though I've many teachers, my capacity for pledges remains
    weak;
though I've many students, my patience and will to help are
    scant.
Dance and trample on the head of this betrayer, false conception!
Mortally strike at the heart of this butcher and enemy, Ego!

61

Though I make promises readily, my actual assistance is scant;
though my fame may be great, when I am probed, even gods
    and ghosts are appalled.
Dance and trample on the head of this betrayer, false conception!
Mortally strike at the heart of this butcher and enemy, Ego!

62

Though I am weak in learning, my temerity for empty words
    is great;
though slight in scriptural knowledge, I meddle in all kinds of
    topics.
Dance and trample on the head of this betrayer, false conception!
Mortally strike at the heart of this butcher and enemy, Ego!

63

Though I may have many friends and servants, none is
    dedicated;
though I may have many leaders, none is a guardian I can rely on.

Dance and trample on the head of this betrayer, false
  conception!
Mortally strike at the heart of this butcher and enemy, Ego!

64
Though my status may be high, my qualities are less than a
  ghost's;
though I may be a great teacher, my afflictions are worse than
  a demon's.
Dance and trample on the head of this betrayer, false
  conception!
Mortally strike at the heart of this butcher and enemy, Ego!

65
Though my views may be lofty, my deeds are worse than a
  dog's;
though my qualities may be numerous, the fundamental ones
  are lost to the winds.
Dance and trample on the head of this betrayer, false
  conception!
Mortally strike at the heart of this butcher and enemy, Ego!

66
I nurture all my self-centered desires deep within;
in all disputes I blame others with no basis.
Dance and trample on the head of this betrayer, false
  conception!
Mortally strike at the heart of this butcher and enemy, Ego!

67
Though clad in saffron robes, I seek protection from the
  ghosts;
though I've taken the precepts, my conduct is that of a demon.

Dance and trample on the head of this betrayer, false conception!
Mortally strike at the heart of this butcher and enemy, Ego!

68
Though the gods create my happiness, I propitiate malevolent
  spirits;
though the Dharma acts as my savior, I deceive the Three
  Jewels—
Dance and trample on the head of this betrayer, false conception!
Mortally strike at the heart of this butcher and enemy, Ego!

69
Though always living in solitude, I am carried away by
  distractions;
though receiving sublime scriptures, I cherish divination and
  shamanism.[139]
Dance and trample on the head of this betrayer, false conception!
Mortally strike at the heart of this butcher and enemy, Ego!

70
Forsaking ethical discipline, the liberation path, I cling to
  paternal home;
casting my happiness into the river, I chase after misery.
Dance and trample on the head of this betrayer, false
  conception!
Mortally strike at the heart of this butcher and enemy, Ego!

71
Forsaking the gateway to liberation, I wander in the wilderness;[140]
though I've obtained a precious human birth, I seek the hell
  realms.
Dance and trample on the head of this betrayer, false conception!
Mortally strike at the heart of this butcher and enemy, Ego!

72

Putting aside spiritual developments, I pursue the profits of
   trade;
leaving my teacher's classroom behind, I roam through towns
   and places.
Dance and trample on the head of this betrayer, false
   conception!
Mortally strike at the heart of this butcher and enemy, Ego!


73

Forsaking my own livelihood, I rob others of their
   resources;
squandering my own inherited wealth, I plunder from others.
Dance and trample on the head of this betrayer, false
   conception!
Mortally strike at the heart of this butcher and enemy, Ego!


74

Alas! Though my endurance for meditation is poor, I've sharp
   clairvoyance;[141]
though I've not even reached the edge of the path, my legs are
   needlessly fast.
Dance and trample on the head of this betrayer, false
   conception!
Mortally strike at the heart of this butcher and enemy, Ego!


75

When someone gives useful advice, I view him as a hostile foe;
when someone fools me with treachery, I repay the heartless
   one with kindness.
Dance and trample on the head of this betrayer, false
   conception!
Mortally strike at the heart of this butcher and enemy, Ego!

76

When people treat me as family, I reveal their secrets to their
   foes;
when they befriend me, I thoughtlessly betray their trust.
Dance and trample on the head of this betrayer, false conception!
Mortally strike at the heart of this butcher and enemy, Ego!

77

My ill temper is intense, my paranoia more coarse than
   everyone's;
hard to befriend, I constantly provoke others' negative traits.
Dance and trample on the head of this betrayer, false conception!
Mortally strike at the heart of this butcher and enemy, Ego!

78

When someone asks for favor, I ignore him yet covertly cause
   him harm;
when someone respects my wishes, I don't concur but seek
   disputes from afar.
Dance and trample on the head of this betrayer, false conception!
Mortally strike at the heart of this butcher and enemy, Ego!

79

I dislike advice and am always difficult to be with;
I am easily offended, and my grudge is always strong.
Dance and trample on the head of this betrayer, false conception!
Mortally strike at the heart of this butcher and enemy, Ego!

80

I crave high status and regard sublime beings as foes;
because my lust is strong, I eagerly pursue the young.
Dance and trample on the head of this betrayer, false conception!
Mortally strike at the heart of this butcher and enemy, Ego!

81

Because of fickleness I cast far away my past friendships;
infatuated with novelty, I talk animatedly to everyone.
Dance and trample on the head of this betrayer, false conception!
Mortally strike at the heart of this butcher and enemy, Ego!

82

Having no clairvoyance, I resort to lies and deprecation;
having no compassion, I betray others' trust and cause their
    hearts pain.
Dance and trample on the head of this betrayer, false conception!
Mortally strike at the heart of this butcher and enemy, Ego!

83

Though my learning is feeble, I guess wildly about everything;
as my scriptural knowledge is scant, I engender wrong
    views about everything.
Dance and trample on the head of this betrayer, false conception!
Mortally strike at the heart of this butcher and enemy, Ego!

84

Habituated to attachment and anger, I insult all those who
    oppose me;
habituated to envy, I slander and denigrate others.
Dance and trample on the head of this betrayer, false conception!
Mortally strike at the heart of this butcher and enemy, Ego!

85

Failing to study, I have forsaken the vast [scholarly
    disciplines];
failing to rely upon teachers, I defame the scriptures.
Dance and trample on the head of this betrayer, false conception!
Mortally strike at the heart of this butcher and enemy, Ego!

86

Instead of teaching the discourses, I expound lies of my own
invention;
failing to cultivate pure perception, I utter insults and threats.
Dance and trample on the head of this betrayer, false
conception!
Mortally strike at the heart of this butcher and enemy, Ego!

87

Refusing to condemn deeds that are contrary to Dharma,
I level various criticisms against all well-spoken words.[142]
Dance and trample on the head of this betrayer, false
conception!
Mortally strike at the heart of this butcher and enemy, Ego!

88

Failing to regard signs of disgrace as a source of shame,
I perversely hold what are signs of honor as a source of shame.
Dance and trample on the head of this betrayer, false
conception!
Mortally strike at the heart of this butcher and enemy, Ego!

89

Failing to pursue any suitable deeds,
I perform instead all that is inappropriate.
Dance and trample on the head of this betrayer, false conception!
Mortally strike at the heart of this butcher and enemy, Ego!

90

Powerful one, you who possess the Sugata's dharmakāya
and destroy the demon of egoistic view,
O wielder of club, the weapon of no-self wisdom,
twirl it over your head three times, without hesitation!

91

With your great ferocity obliterate this enemy!
With your great wisdom dismantle this false conception!
With your great compassion protect me from my karma!
Help destroy this Ego once and for all!

92

Whatever suffering exists for the beings in cyclic existence,
pile it all decisively upon this self-grasping.
Wherever the poisons of five afflictions are found,
heap them decisively upon that which shares the same
    nature.

93

Though having thus recognized the root of all evil
through critical reasoning and beyond any doubt,
if I continue to abet it and act in its defense,
then destroy the very person, the grasper himself!

94

Now I will banish all the blames to one source,
and to all beings I'll contemplate their great kindness.[143]
I will take into myself the undesirable qualities of others
and dedicate my virtuous roots for the benefit of all beings.

95

Thus, as I take on myself all [negative] deeds of others
committed through their three doors throughout all three
    times,
so, like a peacock with colorful feathers because of poison,
may the afflictions be transformed into factors of
    enlightenment.

96

As I offer my roots of virtue to sentient beings,
like the crow that has consumed poison and is cured by
    its antidote,
may I hold the lifeline of liberation of all beings
and swiftly attain buddhahood of one gone to bliss.

97

Until all who have been my parents and I have attained
full enlightenment in the Akaniṣṭha realm,
as we wander the six realms due to our karma,
may we all hold each other in our hearts.

98

During that period, even for the sake of only a single being,
may I immerse myself in the three lower realms,
and without compromising the conduct of a great
    bodhisattva,
may I relieve the sufferings of the lower realms.

99

At that very instant, may the guardians of hells
relate to me as their spiritual teacher,
and may their weapons turn into a cascade of flowers;
and free of harms, may peace and happiness prevail.

100

May the beings of the lower realms, too, obtain clairvoyance
    and mantra,
and may they attain human or celestial birth and generate the
    awakening mind;
may they take me as their teacher and rely upon me,
and may they repay my kindness through spiritual practice.

101

At this time, too, may all the beings of the higher realms
meditate thoroughly on no-self just like me,
and without contrasting existence and pacification,[144]
may they meditate on their perfect equanimity;
may they recognize their self-identity as perfect equanimity.

102

If I do this, the enemy will be vanquished!
If I do this, false conceptions will be vanquished!
I'll meditate on the nonconceptual wisdom of no-self.
So why would I not attain the causes and effects of a buddha's
    form body?

103

Listen! All of this is but dependent origination.
Dependent and empty, they are devoid of self-subsistence.
Changing from one form into another, they are like
    apparitions;
like a fire ring [seen in a rotating torch], they are mere
    illusions.

104

Like the plantain tree, life force has no inner core;
like a bubble, life has no inner core;
like a mist, it dissipates when you look down;
like a mirage, it beguiles from a distance;
like a reflection in a mirror, it appears tangible and real;
like a fog, it appears as if it is here to stay.

105

This butcher and enemy, Ego, too, is just the same:
though it is often said to exist, it never does;

though seemingly real, nowhere is it really;
though appearing, it's beyond proof and refutation.

106
So how can there be a wheel of karma?
It's thus: Though they are devoid of intrinsic existence,
just as moon's reflection appears in a cup of water,
karma and its effects appear as diverse falsehoods.
So within this mere appearance I will follow the ethical
    norms.

107
When the fire at the end of the universe blazes in a dream,
I am terrified by its heat, though it has no intrinsic reality.
Likewise, although hell realms and their likes have no intrinsic
    reality,
out of trepidation for being smelted, burned, and so on,
    I forsake evil.

108
When in feverish delirium, although there is no darkness
    at all,
one feels as if plunged and trapped inside a deep, dark cave.
So, too, although ignorance and so on lack intrinsic reality,
I will dispel ignorance by means of the three wisdoms.[145]

109
When a musician plays a song on his fiddle,
the sound, if probed, reveals no intrinsic reality.
Nonetheless melodious tunes arise through aggregation of
    unprobed facts
and soothe the anguish that lies in people's hearts.

110

Likewise when karma and its effects are thoroughly analyzed,
though they do not exist as intrinsically one or many,
vividly appearing, they cause the rising and cessation of
   phenomena.
Seemingly real, they bring every experience of birth and
   death.
So within this mere appearance I'll follow the ethical norms.


111

When drops of water fill a vase,
it is neither the first drop that fills it
nor the last drop or any drop individually;
the vase is filled through a gathering of dependent factors.


112

Likewise, when someone experiences joy and suffering—
   the effects—
this is not due to the first instant of their cause,
and nor is it due to the last instant of the cause.
Joy and pain are felt through the coming together of
   dependent factors.
So within this mere appearance I will observe ethical norms.


113

Ah! So utterly delightful when left unanalyzed,
this world of appearance, devoid of any essence,
seems as if it really does exist.
Profound indeed is this truth so hard for the weak to see.


114

Now as I place my mind on this truth in total equipoise,
what is there that retains definite appearance?

What exists and what does not exist?
What thesis is there anywhere of *is* or *is not*?

115
There is no object, no subject, nor no ultimate nature;
free of all ethical norms and conceptual elaborations,
if I abide naturally with this uncontrived awareness
in the ever-present, innate state, I will become a great being.

116
Thus by practicing conventional awakening mind
and the ultimate mind of awakening,
may I accomplish without obstacles the two
    accumulations
and realize perfect fulfillment of the two aims.

## Colophon

This text entitled *The Wheel Weapon Striking at the Vital Points
of the Enemy* was composed by the great Dharmarakṣita, a yogi
of scriptural knowledge, reasoning, and realizations, in accordance with the instructions of the sublime teachers. He composed this in a jungle where terrifying animals of prey roam
free, and he undertook its practice in the terrifying jungle of
our degenerate era.

He gave this teaching to Atiśa, who in order to transform
many sentient beings so difficult to tame, undertook this practice throughout all places where sentient beings lie, whether in
cardinal or intermediate directions. As he experienced the realizations of this practice, he uttered the following lines:

> When I renounced my kingdom and practiced austerity,
> I accumulated merit and met with my supreme teacher.

He revealed to me this sublime Dharma nectar and
initiated me into it.
Having mastered the antidotes today, I commit the
words to my heart.

By casting wide my intelligence free of prejudice
upon a detailed study of diverse doctrinal systems,
I have witnessed immeasurable wonders,
but I've found this teaching most helpful to our
degenerate age.

From among his countless disciples in India and Tibet, Atiśa
bestowed this teaching to the most qualified vessel, Upāsaka
[Dromtönpa], who was prophesied by many meditation deities
such as the Bhagavatī Tārā. This teaching was given to help
tame the hardened people of Tibet, a land outside the bounds
of civilization. The father conqueror [Atiśa] and his son
[Dromtönpa] themselves acted as the scholar and translator of
this text.

Atiśa [gave this teaching] to Dromtönpa, [who then transmitted it] to Potowa, and thence, in a lineal order, to Sharawa,
Chekawa, Chilbupa, Lha Chenpo, Lha Drowai Gönpo, Öjopa,
Khenpo Martön, Khenpo Sherap Dorjé, Buddharatna, Kīrtiśīla, Gyalwa Sangpo, Nup Chölungpa Sönam Rinchen, and he
to myself, Shönu Gyalchok Könchok Bang.

This belongs to the cycle of Dharmarakṣita's mind training
teachings.

# A VAJRA SONG

LIKE OUR PREVIOUS entry, the precise origin of this short text entitled *Melodies of an Adamantine Song* remains a source of intrigue. Traditionally, the work is attributed to one Maitrīyogi, also known as Kusalī Jr., one of Atiśa's three Indian teachers of mind training. We know very little of this master, other than the scant personal information we find in some of the later Tibetan biographical writings on Atiśa. According to these sources, Kusalī Jr. was a yogi dedicated to the cultivation of bodhisattva Maitreya, the future Buddha, from which he acquired the epithet Maitrīyogi, or "practitioner of loving-kindness." The same sources also tell us that this master's empathic power was so great, once he even felt the pain of a dog that was being hit by a stick, with clear bluish marks visible on his back.

Although reference to the person of Maitrīyogi is found in earlier Kadam texts, such as Sé Chilbu's commentary on the *Seven-Point Mind Training*, to date, I have yet to see any explicit mention of this particular text in any work before the late fourteenth or early fifteenth century. The earliest we have is the inclusion of the full text in Shönu Gyalchok's *Compendium of Well-Uttered Insights*, where, in the colophon, we find the following statement: "This sublime being [Atiśa] gave this instruction both in India and Tibet as a hidden guide to those sublime ones who shared deep interest in the practice." Unfortunately, Shönu Gyalchok does not tell us what source he used when compiling his anthology. Shönu Gyalchok's version is clearly the one we find in *Mind Training: The Great Collection*, the basis of the translation below.

Unlike *Wheel of Sharp Weapons*, we do not have any traditional exposition in the form of commentary on this short text. Ostensibly, the work is a series of ecstatic, spontaneous songs sung in a dialogue between Maitrīyogi and Maitreya. A third voice, an anonymous narrator, is probably the person who first compiled the songs into a single narrative.

The text is composed of three parts. First is a song expressing deep commitment to the altruistic ideals of taking others' suffering upon oneself and offering one's virtues to others, culminating with a statement of a single-pointed determination to have one's mind trained. At the end of this song, the text refers to the preceding verses as "a chanting meditation (*gyer sgom*) on compassion, loving-kindness, and awakening mind in the form of an adamantine, or *vajra*, song," the suggestion here being that this is a meditation practice to be undertaken in the form of chanting.

In response to this song, the bodhisattva Maitreya utters a series of lines expressing his joy at the yogi's dedication and practice. Opening with the lines:

> This song that dispels sufferings of the lower realms
>   through mere hearing,
> this song that cuts down the tree of cyclic existence
>   through mere reflection,
> this song that swiftly grants enlightenment through
>   mere meditation—
> wondrous indeed is this song of love, compassion, and
>   awakening mind!

Maitreya extols the virtue of engaging in the altruistic practices enshrined in *tonglen* practice and states that there is nothing in the Mahayana scriptures that is not contained within this spiritual practice. This is the second part of the text.

The final part of the text opens with a description of a host of miraculous beneficial effects that result from this exchange between the yogi and his meditation deity, which then leads to Maitreya revealing his entire form to the yogi. This is followed by the final prayers honoring Maitreya through making a series of offerings to him, concluding with an appeal to help the yogi have his mind successfully trained.

# 10. Melodies of an Adamantine Song: A Chanting Meditation on Mind Training

*Attributed to Maitrīyogi*

Alas! To guide all beings who've been my parents,
I'll extract without exception the five poisons of each being
by means of the five poisonous afflictions present in me;
whatever virtue I may possess, such as an absence of
    attachment,
I will distribute equally to all beings of the six realms.

Using the painful fruits of my karma, such as sickness and so on,
I will extract all similar sufferings of sentient beings;
whatever joy and benefit I may possess, such as absence of
    illness,
I will distribute equally to all beings of the six realms.

If I do this, what occasion is there for me, even for a single
    instant,
to wander aimlessly in this ocean of cyclic existence?
Yet until I have attained full enlightenment,
whatever class of the five poisons and their fruits may lie
    in store,
I will exhaust entirely in this very lifetime.

I will extract them this very year and this very month;
I will exhaust them this very day and this very instant;

I will seek the means to cut even the thread of minor
    sufferings.
O Maitrīyogi, make sure that your mind becomes trained![146]

I, Maitrīyogi, regularly recite this song, wherein loving-kindness,
compassion, and awakening mind are sung as a vajra song, and on
one occasion, near the river Ganges, Bhagavan Maitreya, the
embodiment of great compassion, appeared in the form of a king
and approached me. He then uttered the following lines:

This song that dispels sufferings of the lower realms through
    mere hearing,
this song that cuts down the tree of cyclic existence through
    mere reflection,
this song that swiftly grants enlightenment through mere
    meditation—
wondrous indeed is this song of love, compassion, and
    awakening mind!

Though the five poisonous afflictions must be destroyed as
    enemies,
amazing indeed that you still uphold them in your heart!
Though sickness and suffering are hard to endure in all
    respects,
amazing indeed is your current way of being!

Who would not find it hard to wander through samsara
    selflessly
by discarding self-interest and embracing others' well-being?
So to take others' misfortune upon yourself without being
    tied
by thoughts of self-interest even for an instant is sublime
    indeed!

Though the Mahayana scriptures are numberless,
not even an atom-sized portion is missing from this teaching.
So this vajra song of yours, O yogi,
whether it's heard, reflected upon, expounded, or meditated
    upon,
is a sublime refuge for the entire world, including the gods.

Wondrous indeed that the innermost essence of the mind
of the buddhas of all ten directions shines within you!

As [Maitreya] uttered these lines in response to the words of
the vajra song, Maitrīyogi experienced great ecstasy, and with
the knots of his doubts undone, he entered the great battle of
the heroic ones. *Kye ho!*

Furthermore, as [Maitrīyogi] trained his mind in this spiritual
practice three times in the day and three times at night, with
full mindfulness of time and context, and free of forgetfulness,
singing this vajra song to rejuvenate his elements, like a mother
who loves her only son, all the gods, yakṣas, smell-eaters,
demi-gods, garuḍas, semihumans, the great belly-crawlers,
flesh-eating demons, ogres, and so on were brought under his
influence and revered him. Similarly, the king of the land, his
ministers, his queens, the brahman priests, householders,
young men and women, ordinary people, and so on, came
under his influence as well. They joyfully followed him, and
anyone who saw this or heard of this became endowed with loving nature. Horses, elephants, water buffaloes, monkeys,
winged creatures, waterborne creatures, mountain creatures,
predators, all beings of the six classes, including even small
insects like the ants, remained unafraid of him, and peacefully
they converged in the presence of the yogi.

Then the yogi felt, "I cultivated in my heart love, compassion, and awakening mind; I have recited the words as incantations and have sung the melodious vajra song. Because of this Blessed Maitreya, the embodiment of great compassion, revealed bare his face to me and uttered words of delight, which severed the entire matrix of doubts. As a consequence, my practices of forbearance, joyous effort, and so on became enhanced like a waxing moon. By the force of this, like a mother gazing on her only son, all beings of the six classes became pleased with me."

In grateful response, and with thoughts of making offerings to Buddha Maitreya, Maitrīyogi sang this song:

Those closely related to me since beginningless time,
all sentient beings who've been my parents,
I recall my pledge to lead them to supreme enlightenment.
I make offerings to Maitreya with this spiritual practice.

Then, not entangled in self-interest for even an instant,
I contemplate in my heart others' welfare alone—
this is the principal cause for attaining full enlightenment.
I make offerings to Maitreya with this spiritual practice.

Whatever experiences I may undergo—joyful, painful, or
    neutral—
I will eagerly embrace them as aids to enlightenment.
Whatever merits I may accumulate over many eons,
I will prevent them from ripening as the śrāvaka's cowardly
    path.
I make offerings to Maitreya with this spiritual practice.

Whatever undesirable events may befall me on such
    occasions,
may my armor of forbearance never be lost for even an instant.

Even if someone I've nurtured with kindness
acts against me ungratefully, I will nurture him with a
    smiling face.
I make offerings to Maitreya with this spiritual practice.

Though the hateful, on their part, engage in negative acts,
may I never give in to negative thoughts for even an
    instant.
Even should the entire universe rise up as demons, ghosts,
    or enemies,
I will never guard the binding chains of self-centeredness.
I make offerings to Maitreya with this spiritual practice.

Even when afflicted with an illness certain to kill me,
I will not entrust myself to nonvirtuous acts.
Though my resources may be meager because of my habit
    of miserliness,
I will never place my hope in an unwholesome livelihood.
I make offerings to Maitreya with this spiritual practice.

Even when surrounded by negative companions,
I will never forsake the resolution of the remedies.
In brief, whatever I do—going, sitting, and so on—
I will never act without careful examination.
I make offerings to Maitreya with this spiritual practice.

Though this is so, not even an atom has ever existed
that has been affirmed to be substantially real.
This, then, is the principal cause for attaining enlightenment.
I make offerings to Maitreya with this spiritual practice.

Through this sublime offering of meditative practice
to help train this yogi's mind,

O soldiers of loving-kindness,
Accept this offering and help transform my mind.

As this offering was made, the five offering goddesses appeared in space with an infinity of diverse offerings, such as music, lights, and other attractive objects. At that moment, the sublime masters who have trained their mind in Mahayana recognized this spiritual practice as a source of great wonder. They observed that although many have engaged in the austerity of this spiritual practice—received the teaching and undertaken its practice—[it was Maitrīyogi who] gave the instruction to Atiśa. He was the master of 108 extremely holy places, the crown jewel among fifty-two learned pandits, a heroic being venerated by sixty-two religious kings, the preceptor of countless upholders of ethical discipline (*vinaya*), the teacher of countless upholders of scriptural discourses (*sūtra*), an object of reverence by numberless upholders of higher knowledge (*abhidharma*), and the spiritual mentor of oceans of knowledge bearers (*vidyādhara*)—in brief, he is an unrivaled sublime being and the protector of all sentient beings. This embodiment of great compassion undertook the practice [of this teaching]. This is as stated in the following lines:

> He who discards his own interests and spontaneously accomplishes
> the welfare of others, he is my spiritual teacher.

This sublime being gave this instruction both in India and Tibet as a hidden guide to those sublime ones who shared deep interest in the practice.

As for its lineage: Maitreya, Maitrīyogi, who in turn transmitted it to Master Atiśa.

# TRANSFORMING ADVERSITY

THE NEXT TWO texts address the mind training practice of taking adversities and afflictions into the path to awakening.

*A Teaching on Taking Afflictions onto the Path* presents the instruction of taking upon oneself all the afflictions, such as attachment and aversion, of other sentient beings and on this basis engaging in the cultivation of the two awakening minds, conventional and ultimate. We have no information about the author of this short text, nor do we have any knowledge of the transmission lineage of this particular instruction.

*Mind Training Taking Joys and Pains onto the Path* is a text, as the colophon of the text itself states, based on a well-known single-verse mind training composed by the Kashmiri pandit Śākyaśrībhadra (1127–1225). This Kashmiri master came to Tibet at the beginning of the thirteenth century and, among other things, became a teacher of Sakya Paṇḍita. This fascinating short text on mind training employs the well-known Vajrayana meditation of taking death, intermediate state, and rebirth onto the path as the three buddha bodies. The text provides an instruction on how to apply this three-buddha-bodies meditation for the specifically mind training objective of taking everyday experience as a spiritual path.

# 11. A Teaching on Taking Afflictions onto the Path

Homage to the Precious Teachers!

IT IS SAID that the instruction for transforming intense mental states, such as attachment and aversion, into the path on the basis of the two awakening minds—how to take afflictions onto the path—is presented in the tantras. It is impossible, however, for the ordinary afflictions themselves to become the path. As far as taking afflictions onto the path by means of selecting them as your meditation focus and turning them away is concerned, this has been taught repeatedly in the sutras. The instruction for this sutra approach is as follows.

Take attachment, for instance. First, when you observe yourself experiencing attachment to either an internal experience or to a specific external object, contemplate the following: "This is the affliction of attachment. If not relinquished, not purified, and not conquered, it will give rise to immeasurable suffering, such as birth in the lower realms. If transformed and conquered, it can become a condition for full enlightenment. I will therefore conquer it so that it becomes a condition for buddhahood."

Thinking thus, take in to your mind your enemies' afflictions of attachment. Then, as you do when meditating on loving-kindness, cultivate this toward a larger group. Finally, take upon yourself all the attachments, along with their propensities, existing in all beings. As you do this, imagine that your own attachment becomes so great as to be unfathomable. Imagine that all sentient beings become free of attachment and attain buddhahood. This is the [practice of taking afflictions upon yourself on the basis of the] conventional awakening mind.

Take upon yourself this attachment of yours, the size of Mount Meru, and heap others' attachment upon it as well. Then reflect, "Attachment is by nature mental; apart from the mind there is no attachment, not even an atom's breadth. So when the mind observes itself, past and future states become no more. The past has ceased to be, while the future is, though subject to cessation, yet to be, and the present is devoid of any identifiable characteristics, such as shape and color. Not existing in any manner, the mind abides like space. So what is called *attachment* is a mere name with no referent at all." Place your mind in this state as long as it abides. This is the practice of the ultimate awakening mind.

From these two, respectively, arise the form body (*rūpa-kāya*), the mere hearing of whose name gives rise to the enlightened activities that help pacify the afflictions, and the dharmakāya, which helps eliminate all afflictions and their propensities, which lead to more contaminated states. We should know how to extend this practice similarly to all afflictions, such as hatred, the master said.

This has been written on the basis of my teacher's words alone, with no omissions or additions. May the goodness of the content of this extremely profound instruction for taking afflictions onto the path equal the measure of space!

# 12. Mind Training Taking Joys and Pains onto the Path

Homage to the spiritual teachers!

FOR THIS INSTRUCTION on taking joys and pains onto the path, you should first generate the awakening mind. Then, when experiencing joy, identify clearly what it is that experiences the joy—whether it is your body or your mind. Since your physical body is like a corpse, it cannot exist as the enjoyer of that happiness. Yet the mind is empty like the sky, and as such, it is devoid of itself, so it too cannot be the enjoyer of that joy. Therefore, since that which conceives of joy is devoid of itself, recognize what is empty as empty. Then place your mind—lucid, pure, relaxed, and settled—for as long as you can in this expanse of emptiness. This is the method for attaining the uncontrived, uncontaminated dharmakāya, the buddha body of reality.

While in this state, vividly conceive what you experience as joy to be in essence your meditation deity; and regardless of whether your mind is distracted, seal yourself inseparably with your meditation deity. This is the method for attaining the enjoyment body (*saṃbhogakāya*), which is the means for taming the pure trainees.[147]

Not divorced from this identity, dedicate what you perceive

as joy for the benefit of all sentient beings and recite the following three times:

> **When happy, I will dedicate my virtues to all;**
> **may benefit and happiness pervade all of space!**[148]

This is the method for attaining the emanation body (*nirmāṇ-akāya*), which is the means for taming the impure trainees.[149]

Now if you experience pain, vividly identify what it is that experiences the suffering—whether it is your body or your mind. Since your physical body is like a corpse, it cannot exist as the subject of suffering. Yet the mind is empty like the sky; as such, it is devoid of itself, so it too cannot be the subject of that suffering. Then affirm the emptiness of that which conceives of suffering to be devoid of itself, and place your mind—lucid, pure, relaxed, and settled—for as long as you can in this expanse of emptiness. This is the method for attaining the uncontrived, uncontaminated dharmakāya.

While in this state, vividly contemplate what you conceive of as suffering to be in essence your meditation deity; and regardless of whether your mind is distracted, seal yourself inseparably with your meditation deity. This is the method for attaining the enjoyment body, which is the means for taming the pure trainees.

Not divorced from this identity, dedicate what you perceive as suffering for the benefit of sentient beings and recite the following three times:

> **When suffering, I will take on the pains of all beings;**
> **may the ocean of suffering become dry!**

This is the method for attaining the emanation body, which is the means for taming the impure trainees.

This, then, is the instruction for taking joy and suffering onto the path.

The lineage of this is as follows: Paṇchen Śākyaśrī, Trophu Lotsāwa, Khenchen Lhodrakpa, Khenchen Dewa Jamchenpa, Rinchen Drakpa Shenyen, Chöjé Sönam Rinchen, and Shönu Gyalchok.

# NEW ATTITUDES

THE FIRST OF the next three texts, *Sumpa Lotsāwa's Ear-Whispered Mind Training*, develops the intriguing theme of how to sustain a state of mind that is carefree yet joyful. Shönu Gyalchok identifies the root text of this work to be the following four-line stanza, which he attributes to Sumpa Lotsāwa:

> If you can tolerate anything, whatever you do brings happiness;
> if your mind rests where it's placed, you can journey anywhere;
> if your mind is fused with Dharma, it's okay even if you die;
> if you have recognized the mind as unborn, there is no death.

Something similar to these four lines is cited in the text.

So far I have failed to locate any significant information on the life of Sumpa Lotsāwa. In the information on the transmission of the lineage at the end of this short work, it says that Sumpa Lotsāwa himself transmitted the instruction of this practice to the famous Tibetan master Sakya Paṇḍita. Furthermore, there is a brief reference to Sumpa Lotsāwa as Dharma Yönten in *The Blue Annals*,[150] where he is listed as having translated several important texts composed by the Indian master

Jayasena, from whom the Sakya patriarch Drakpa Gyaltsen received teachings as well. This would place Sumpa Lotsāwa between late twelfth and early thirteenth century, which fits well with the time of Sakya Paṇḍita. As to the identity of the author of this mind training text based on Sumpa Lotsāwa's instructions, the question must remain open.

*Bodhisattva Samantabhadra's Mind Training* focuses on what kind of attitudes and basic outlook are essential for a successful practice of mind training. It speaks of cultivating the "expansive thought," the "resolute thought," and the "diamond-like thought." Shönu Gyalchok characterizes this work as supplemental instructions to the practice of giving and taking by means of training the mind in the conventional awakening mind.

Judging by its literary style, especially the frequent use of the expression "it was taught," we can safely conclude that this text belongs to the genre of *sindri*, lecture notes taken at an oral teaching. According to the colophon, that teaching was given by one Mipham Chöjé, which is the Tibetan version of Ajita (Maitreya). This would then explain the significance of the opening salutation, where the author pays homage to his teacher Maitreya. He is probably the fourteenth-century Kadam/Sakya master Tsültrim Dar, who is sometimes referred to as the second Maitreya. The lineage of instruction presented here seems to be one steming from Atiśa through to Drom-tönpa and their disciple Gönpawa Wangchuk Gyaltsen (1016–82) and onward through Master Neusurpa (1042–1118).

According to Shönu Gyalchok, the next two short texts, *Mind Training Removing Obstacles* and *Mahayana Mind Training Eliminating Future Adversities*, actually constitute a single text. Interestingly, in the colophon of this second work, there is the short statement that the instructions contained here stem from Atiśa, but no further information of the subsequent lineage of its transmission is given. Although the instructions themselves are rooted in early sources, the texts seem to point toward Shönu Gyalchok himself as being the author.

The two short texts address the theme of how to deal with life's inevitable ups and downs and transform adversities into opportunities for spiritual growth. The specific thought processes presented in these two texts, especially the latter, echo some of the key themes from *Leveling Out All Conceptions*. The key concern in this text appears to be to ensure how best to prevent future circumstances from undermining our practice, and more importantly, how best to prevent the arising of afflictions before they reach a potentially destructive level. Furthermore, unlike other mind training texts, here the practice of giving and taking, *tonglen*, which is the heart of mind training, is presented in the concluding section of the instruction as part of the benefits. This is done on the basis of a four-line stanza, the source of which I have so far failed to identify.

# 13. Sumpa Lotsāwa's Ear-Whispered Mind Training

Homage to the spiritual teachers!

THE REALIZED SIDDHA Sumpa Lotsāwa traveled to India and undertook extensive study of most of the secret mantra systems. Just before his return to Tibet, he brought his leftover gold to offer to the great enlightenment monument at Bodhgaya. As he was circumambulating this stupa, two women, one reddish and the other bluish, were circumambulating the stupa as well; at times they hovered above in the sky, and at other times they appeared to be walking on the ground.

The bluish woman then said to the reddish one, "Last night I felt mentally restless; I felt like going somewhere. I hope this is not some premonition about my death, for I am terrified of dying." Exclaiming this, she asked her companion four questions. To this, the reddish woman, casting side glances at Lotsāwa, responded to her companion as follows:

1. If you have a sense of abandonment, O lady, everything you do will bring happiness. Your mind suffers because it lacks this quality of abandonment.
2. If your mind rests where it is placed, O lady, it will be okay even if you travel elsewhere. Your mind suffers because it cannot rest where it is placed.

3. If your mind is turned to Dharma, O lady, you can die with ease. Your mind suffers because it is not usually turned to Dharma.

4. If you have recognized your mind as unborn, O lady, there will be no death. Your mind suffers because you have failed to recognize your mind as unborn.

She was said to have responded to her companion with these four statements. At that point it is said that Lotsāwa overcame his sadness, the practices he had learned in the past became effective, and extraordinary realizations arose in his mind.

The following is the introduction to this practice:

It is taught that if you have a sense of acceptance, you will be content with whatever material resources you have commensurate with the [karmic potential] you have stored for yourself. You will not envy others' prosperity, and you will ensure that your immediate circumstances, whether happy or painful, will not burden your heart. You need to recognize the nature of your own mind, guard your own place, and attain freedom on the basis of blessings from your spiritual teachers and on the basis of applying special meditation techniques. The fusion of your mind with Dharma is this very lucid awareness of yours; it is vital that you recognize its true nature. To realize the mind as unborn is to realize its origination and to cease its death. The realization where you no longer differentiate between the actual meditation session and periods between sessions as concerns the cognition of mind as free of origination, cessation, and abiding—this realization has no death.

The lineage of this teaching is that the most holy Vajravārāhī and two Tārās revealed it to Sumpa Lotsāwa, he to Sakya Paṇḍita, he to the great siddha Tsotrangwa, he to Khedrup Chöjé, he to

Ritrö Rechen, he to Prajñābodhi, he to Dönshakpa Buddharatna, he to Kīrtiśīla, he to Chöjé Gyalwa Sangpo, he to Chöjé Sönam Rinchen, and he to [me,] Könchok Bang.

# 14. Bodhisattva Samantabhadra's Mind Training

Homage to my teacher Maitreya!

THE TEACHER SAID:

All phenomena are manifestations of your own mind, so you must bring them all together and then engage in your practice. Furthermore, since this lineage of sacred words is the path of your spiritual teacher, recognize that all the offerings of the three times are the creative play of your teacher and engage in the training of your mind. So pay homage to the teacher and make outer, inner, and secret offerings to him and make supplications to him as well. Entrust your tethers to the teacher and then engage in the practices—from [contemplations on] impermanence to the ultimate nature of reality.

For this establish the perfect spacelike view, wherein all phenomena of cyclic existence and beyond are primordially devoid of origination and cessation and transcend all boundaries of conceptual elaboration. Train thus in the skills of noncessation, and cultivate the three [means of developing love, compassion, and the awakening mind]: (1) through focusing on sentient beings, (2) through focusing on mere phenomena, and (3) through objectless focus.[151] Cultivate the three equanimities toward others: equanimity free of discriminating close and distant, equanimity in your level of respect, and equanimity free of discriminating good and bad. Cultivate these three qualities. Furthermore cultivate the "expansive thought," the "resolute thought," and the "diamondlike thought."

## I. Expansive thought

The first refers to some attitudes of the Great Vehicle. As the younger brother generated the aspiration, "May I achieve equality with all my elder brothers, especially in their enlightened activities, such as turning the wheel of Dharma," he attained equality with all. The Buddha Śākyamuni, too, generated the expansive thought, "May I tame all those sentient beings who are unattractive, who possess a negative nature and have failed to become trainees of all the previous buddhas." He then engaged in countless austerities. The teacher spoke also of how, owing to the great compassion of the lords of the three families, the Buddha became the embodiment of the great compassion of all the buddhas. He spoke also of how the Buddha's emanations pervade the entire billionfold universe and how immeasurable are the waves of his great compassion.

When he was born as the bodhisattva Vegadharin, Vajrapāṇi had the thought that the Great Vehicle is not for the swift attainment of buddhahood. So as a bodhisattva he remained always within cyclic existence, endured great hardships to assist suffering sentient beings, and pleased the buddhas through veneration. He realized the qualities of the Buddha and became the custodian of the secrets of all the buddhas of the three times. He then engaged in such expansive conduct as subduing Māra and guarding against the obstacles.

As for Ārya Mañjuśrī, when he first generated the awakening mind, he took a vow to lead all beings to the state of buddhahood while still engaged in bodhisattva deeds. He took the vow that until he had led all sentient beings in all the ten directions to enlightenment and they had individually attained buddha-hood, he would not himself become fully enlightened. He vowed that even for the sake of a single being he would remain until the end, and he vowed that for the sake of every single being, he would never become disheartened by sufferings such as those in the hell of Avīci. Thus he vowed to engage in the enlightened activities of the Buddha even while remaining as a bodhisattva, and he made the aspiration, "May it be a betrayal of the tathāgatas to realize full enlightenment before my vows are fulfilled!" thinking this would be tantamount to committing one of the five heinous acts.

Bodhisattva Samantabhadra was even more expansive than all these bodhisattvas.[152] When he first generated the awakening mind, he did so in a manner that included, without exception, the aspirations of all the buddhas. Also, when engaging in the bodhisattva deeds, he did so by embracing all the austerities, without exception, undertaken by all the bodhisattvas of the three times. He cultivated the aspiration to usher into buddhahood all sentient beings without exception and equal to the limits of space. He vowed that he would perfect the enlightened activities of all the buddhas while still a bodhisattva, and that when he performed in each buddha realm the inconceivable enlightened activities of the respective buddhas, he would undergo such sufferings as those of Avīci for countless eons even for the sake of a single being, and he pledged that he would perform the enlightened deeds of the buddhas of the three times. He generated such altruistic thoughts as, "I shall generate the altruism of the bodhisattvas of the three times that I have not generated so far. I shall endure the austerities associated with conduct that lies beyond the capacity [of many bodhisattvas]." He generated the altruistic intention to lead to the state of buddhahood those sentient beings who had been abandoned even by those with great compassion and skillful means.

By emanating bodies equal in number to all atoms in the universe, he made outer, inner, and secret offerings in the presence of each and every buddha. Each of these bodies cultivated countless buddha realms. Similarly he made aspiration prayers to help discipline those trainees whose conduct is so hard to reign in. He pledged to engage in the enlightened deeds of all the buddhas, and he vowed to try in every single moment to accomplish the activities of all the buddhas of the three times. He prayed, "If I realize buddhahood before these aspirations are fulfilled, may this be betrayal of all the buddhas of the three times." So his courage is as infinite as space and transcends words.

Likewise, you should generate a mind even more expansive than that of the buddhas and bodhisattvas. It is on this basis that the awakening mind will first arise, will abide in the middle, and will finally culminate in buddhahood. Do not become disheartened.

This awakening mind is a catalyst for suffering, a counterbalance to joy, a walking companion for those who are afraid, a remedy for sickness and malevolent harms, and it levels the afflictions flat. To follow in the footsteps of the buddhas and bodhisattvas, perform the following visualization.

At your heart, with yourself in your ordinary form, visualize, evolving from an *A*, a white *Maṃ* on a moon disk. Light rays radiate profusely from this and touch all sentient beings throughout space. The light rays extract karma and afflictions, such as attachment, anger, delusion, pride, envy, and miserliness, as well as the six root and the twenty derivative afflictions. They also extract the negative acts motivated by the afflictions that obstruct higher rebirth and liberation and force beings to experience the sufferings of cyclic existence and the lower realms. These negative acts include the ten negative actions committed through body, speech, and mind, the five heinous acts, the five approximate heinous acts, the root infraction of [bodhisattva] precepts, showing disrespect to the Three Jewels, abandoning the teachings, and belittling the noble beings. Imagine that all of these dissolve into you like rain falling on your body and that the minds of all sentient beings thereby become cleansed and free of obscuration.

Then with the thought "I will purify all this negative karma," visualize another stream of light rays shooting forth that touches all sentient beings. Imagine that all future sufferings of cyclic existence that may harm and afflict their body, speech, and mind—such as the heat and cold of the hell realms, the thirst and hunger of the hungry ghosts, the ignorance and confusion of the animal realms, the conflicts of the demigods, the death and fall of the celestial gods, and the eight and the eleven categories of suffering of the human realm—all these sufferings are dispelled. Imagine that the instant the light rays touch the beings, their bodies and minds become blissful. Then as the light rays dissolve back into your body, imagine that all these sufferings descend upon your body like rain and that every single pore of your body becomes permeated by the inconceivable sufferings of the six realms of existence, such as those of Avīci. Cultivate the thought, "If sentient beings gain freedom from suffering, then what I've taken on as my responsibility will become a truly great task." Reflect further, "Since all sentient beings have placed their trust in me to be their guarantor and protector, I will offer myself as their protector and obtain their release. I will undergo all their sufferings while leading them to happiness."

Now visualize another stream of whitish light rays, which depart and touch the hearts of your teacher and all his lineage, of the buddhas, of the bodhisattvas, of the meditation deities, of the śrāvakas, and of the pratyekabuddhas, drawing forth their obstacles to meditative practice, the damages caused to their body, their failure in realizing their enlightened aspirations, and the disruptions caused to their completion of liberating life deeds. These are visibly drawn forth on the tip of the light rays, which then dissolve into your body like a rain. Then rejoice: "It is indeed a great fortune that I have the honor to shoulder such responsibility."

At all times, never deviate from the spacelike expanse; at all times, never be divorced from contemplating your teachers; offer as gifts to them your body, your wealth, and your roots of virtue. To the obstructive forces who are vengeful and to whom sentient beings owe karmic debts, conjure many effigies of yourself with pleasing appearance and delicious flavor, and offer these to them. Similarly conjure immeasurable meat, blood, bones, internal organs, limbs, and toes and offer these, or whatever they desire, to them. Exhort them to consume these raw if they are in haste, and if not, to devour them cooked. By their eating these, imagine their afflictions of craving are overcome and they experience enhanced bliss. Then make prayers for them to become your disciples in the future.

Some may assert that now is not the time to give [away your body]. However, since guarding this impure body is like carrying a sack of prickly thorns, greater happiness comes if you let go of it, the master said. You should then utter: "As I have accumulated immeasurable merit, through the power of my unsullied intentions and through the blessings of my teachers, may my two accumulations increase immeasurably, and may the enlightened aspirations of all noble beings be fulfilled. May all sentient beings be relieved of suffering and endowed with perfect happiness."

When reciting essence mantras and engaging in wrathful rites, generate yourself as a meditation deity, and through diverse ferocious displays of magical power, crush all mundane bodies into dust and imagine that all beings are led to the wisdom of omniscience. When chronic illness or harmful spells strike you, free of mental agony, cultivate the conviction that they are all without origin. Recognize all experiences as mirror reflections, placing your mind in meditative equipoise on loving-kindness. Thus taught the master.

If afflictions arise in your mind, recognize their nature to be without origin and transform the afflictions into wisdom. Whatever adverse circumstance or conflict may arise, train your mind to transform these into a means for completing the two accumulations. In this manner, then, you partake in everything—food, clothing, and shelter—as factors conducive to the awakening mind. Strive in the causes that help all sentient beings who see, hear, think, or speak about you to exhaust their three obscurations[153] and thus attain the buddha bodies. Take all adverse circumstances onto the perfect path and engage in the deeds of Samantabhadra. Then cultivate the intention, "I shall help realize the enlightened intentions, the enlightened activities, and the aspirations and expansive deeds of all the buddhas and bodhisattvas."

## II. Resolute thought

This refers to cultivating the courage "If fishermen, farmers, and traders can bear the pains of heat and cold [in the course of their work], can't someone like me bear them for the sake of sentient beings' welfare?"[154] With such an attitude, when working for the welfare of other sentient beings, you need to remain resolute and unshaken by negative karma, the afflictions, mundane concerns, the outlook of the Lesser Vehicle, and all forms of grasping at substantial existence, and instead seek omniscience.

## III. Diamondlike thought

This refers to engaging in the practice of the awakening mind uninterrupted by any false conceptions from now until you have attained buddhahood. This, too, must be accomplished through an indivisible union of method and wisdom. When you practice one, the other naturally follows, thus you practice the two in union.

At the time of your full enlightenment, given that the scope and nature of your buddha realm are enlightened qualities that evolve from the distinctive features of your present capacity, strength, and aspirations, then those to whom your loving-kindness extends at present will become your disciples in the future. Therefore, as you cultivate the illusion-like person's awakening mind, endure the austerities, and train in the paths, you will attain full enlightenment in the spacelike expanse and, through your emanations, help free sentient beings from cyclic existence. This is simply a case of space occupying space.

Having thus determined everything as spacelike, recognize everything as expressions of illusion and train in the skills of noncessation, which is the expansive thought of awakening, and thus amass the two illusion-like accumulations. This, then, is the union of method and wisdom. Since the essential points will dawn within, you will not be disheartened by cyclic existence, and you will remain not too far from nirvana, the master said.

At that point, you are free of hopes and fears. Since you have recognized the dharmakāya, even if you descend to the hell of Avīci, you perceive it as the buddha realm of Sukhāvatī. Since you have perceived samsara and nirvana as nondual, you are free of any thoughts of affirmation and abandonment. Since you have perceived buddhas and sentient beings as indivisible, your grasping at good and bad is dismantled. Since you have perceived all phenomena as equal, you are free of biased thoughts such as regarding some to be superior and others infe-rior. So, without deliberately traveling there, you will have arrived at Nāgārjuna's intention!

Those who wish to engage in such spiritual training should, in terms of their actions, gather the accumulations and, in terms of their thoughts, train their minds. They should embrace this practice as their object of admiration and embark on it with deep conviction. Once you have integrated this practice, it will not let you down, and gradually you will gain its realization.

Now, to avoid forgetting the awakening mind throughout all your lives, relinquish the four negative factors and always study to acquire the four positive factors.[155] Train your mind to never desert sentient beings and learn to relinquish the four conditions that lead to such betrayal, which are as follows:

1. If you entertain the thought, "How can I work for the welfare of so many sentient beings?" think instead, "The more there are, the greater my awakening mind will become enhanced."
2. Relinquishing the negative functions: Although it may not be possible to physically befriend all beings, you nonetheless try at all times and gather them mentally.
3. Relinquishing through perceiving the objects of cyclic existence: Just as there are numerous sufferings, you correspondingly eliminate them and remove them [from sentient beings].
4. Relinquishing through perceiving emptiness: If you do not recognize what is empty to be empty and instead grasp at it as substantially real, you suffer. What a pity!

In this manner, relinquish the four conditions that lead you to abandoning [sentient beings] and enhance your compassion for sentient beings as much as possible. When the awakening mind equalizing all sentient beings arises, it is said:

> When the awakening mind has arisen in them,
> instantly the wretched, captives in samsara's prison,

are hailed as children of the sugatas;
they're revered by the worlds of gods and humans.[156]

Such bodhisattvas train to be modest in their desires and content within. In guarding their mindfulness and introspective vigilance, they train just like Ārya Kātyāyana.[157] Those who conduct themselves in the manner of an illusion, because they are free of arrogance, are like mirror reflections of a person. Like one's own hand feeding one's mouth, they are free of any expectation of reward. Like an illusory person, they harbor no hopes of results. Since they have unconditionally given their bodies, wealth, and roots of virtue away, they are said to be like the Buddha.

Although this is not yet the time to actually give [away your body], make sure that your will to give is perfected through pure thought, the master said. In the future, the time will come when, even as a bodhisattva, you will perform the enlightened deeds of the Buddha. Becoming fully enlightened and having attained the dharmakāya (the fulfillment of your own interest), the fulfillment of the welfare of the three fields of beings (pure, impure, and mixed) will take place until the end of cyclic existence through the two form bodies, which constitute the perfection of others' interests.

*Iti.* This has been hidden as a secret.

Master Atiśa gave this teaching to glorious Gönpawa, he to Rinchen Naburpa,[158] then through to Gyergom Sangyé Wön, Sang Gönpa, Khenpo Chöden, Lopön Śhākya Tashi, Gyamapa Tashi Gyaltsen, to Buddharatna, to Kīrtiśīla, to Jayabhadra, to Puṇyaratna, and he to Mipham Chöjé.

# 15. Mind Training Removing Obstacles

Homage to the greatly compassionate spiritual teachers!

DISPELLING OBSTACLES to Mahayana mind training, it has been taught, consists of (1) accepting ill omens as charms, (2) exterminating Māra at his very source, (3) bringing obstacles on to the path, and (4) capping your useless desires.

## 1. First [accepting all ill omens as charms] is as follows:

When worldly people encounter bad omens, such as hearing owls crying or foxes howling, they consult astrology, make divinations, and have rituals performed. You, on the other hand, should eagerly embrace ill omens and negative signs when they appear by cultivating the thought, "Since it is self-grasping that causes me to suffer, may all the suffering that exists in the world arising from the fear of encountering ill omens befall upon this self. May this help vanquish self-grasping."

## 2. Second [exterminating Māra at his very source] is as follows:

It is taught that self-grasping causes us to suffer. So when you experience pain or injury to your body, caused either by humans or by nonhumans, think, "It is this body that causes me to suffer. If you want it, take it away this instant. O king of demons residing above, remove my head! Great indeed is your kindness in causing all the injuries to it. Since you are my ally in subduing the true enemy and my ally in subduing the ghost [of self-grasping], help me exterminate the very continuum of the worldly gods, humans, and ghosts, and help me vanquish this demon to the best of my ability." Cut self-grasping from its root with the thought, "It is not inconsistent [for a mind training practitioner] to relish doing so."

### 3. Third [bringing obstacles onto the path] is as follows:

Whatever unhelpful events, such as physical ailments, mental anxieties, and so on, occur, or when adversities afflict you, contemplate, "This comes from my own self-grasping. If today I do not discard this self-grasping, obstacles will continue to arise. So may all the adversities now in the world and those feared to come be realized upon me. May this help subdue the self and utterly destroy it." Contemplating thus, bring them onto the path.

### 4. Fourth [capping your useless desires] is as follows:

"What benefit has this desire brought me, if any? It has never distanced me from cyclic existence, so it must be destroyed. Then, at least, I will have derived some purpose from its utter uselessness. If I achieve this, it will be due to my teacher's blessing; it will be owing to his kindness. Pray help me so that in the future, too, I can heap upon this self-grasping all useless desires and vanquish them by subjugating them." Contemplating in this way, cap your useless desires.

*Iti.*

# 16. Mahayana Mind Training
## Eliminating Future Adversities

THE MAHAYANA mind training that eliminates future adversities has three parts: [(1) The preliminary, (2) the actual practice, and (3) the purpose of mind training.]

### 1. The preliminary

There are four occasions when mind training is likely to be forgotten: (1) at the agonizing moment of death, (2) in the intermediate state, (3) in the mother's womb, and (4) in the next life. There are four occasions when mind training is likely to be lost: (1) when suffering severe harms at the hands of humans, (2) [when suffering severe harms] caused by nonhumans, (3) when suffering a grave illness brought on by the elements, and (4) when undergoing strong afflictions.

The antidote to these is as follows: Having made offerings to the teacher and the Three Jewels, make the following prayers: "Bless me that undistorted realizations of Mahayana mind training may arise in me. Bless me to not forget mind training during the four occasions when it is likely to be forgotten and to not lose it when it is likely to be lost."

Next, offer tormas to the Dharma protectors and, as before, make aspiration prayers: "Having accumulated the merit, may

Mahayana mind training arise in me. May it not be forgotten when this is likely to occur, and may it not be wasted during the four occasions when this is likely."

Make these aspiration prayers and repeat the same in relation to the collective merit of sentient beings.

The four prescriptions of the practice of Mahayana mind training, the master said, are as follows: (1) all paths are traversed by one, (2) all aspirations are concentrated into one, (3) all conceptions are leveled out, and (4) the remedies are instantly applied to vanquish [the opposing forces].

*All paths are traversed by one*, for there are no enumerations of levels and paths [in mind training]. You simply undermine self-grasping as fully as you can. If you annihilate it today, you attain buddhahood today; if you annihilate it tomorrow, you attain buddhahood tomorrow; if it remains undestroyed, there is no buddhahood; and when you annihilate it, it has been taught, at that instant you become fully enlightened.

*All aspirations are concentrated into one*, for whatever activities you might engage in, be it traveling, strolling, sleeping, or sitting, you have no purpose other than to undermine self-grasping to the best of your ability and to help sentient beings as much as you can. Few other aspirations need be pursued, it has been taught.

*All conceptions are leveled out.* Some assert that all conceptions are to be eliminated; however, you don't need to eliminate them. Take conceptions onto the path instead, for they are the very stuff of the dharmakāya. As for afflictions, they are subtle when they first arise, and it is vital to vanquish them the moment they are born. If not destroyed, they grow enormous and then cannot be overcome. If afflictions can be easily averted by simply applying the antidotes at their first appearance, what a pity if you shy away and don't eliminate them, the master said. So when a conception arises, examine thus: "Where does it arise from? Where does it reside? Where does it go when it ceases?" and recognize that it is devoid of intrinsic existence. And, like meeting a past acquaintance, you take it onto the path, the master said. Or, like snowflakes falling onto hot rocks, you dissolve it into emptiness.

*The remedies are instantly applied to vanquish* [*the opposing forces*], for the instant afflictions arise, just like hitting the head of each pig with a stick, you apply whatever is the most effective antidote [to that specific affliction], the master said.

## 2. The actual practice

The practice of Mahayana mind training has three methods of applying antidotes: (1) conjuring what is not there, (2) vanquishing through direct encounter, and (3) mocking.

The first method is like a Mongol taming a tiger:[159] First he practices by learning the skills of taming a tiger so that when he actually meets a tiger, he can subdue it. If he has not trained previously, he will be unable to tame it and may instead become its prey. Similarly, you should vividly conjure within yourself the powerful afflictions, such as attachment, and then imagine driving them away. By not ignoring your thoughts but training them, the antidotes will appear spontaneously whenever afflictions arise, and because of this you will not be overwhelmed by conditions. In other words, you will not fall under the power of the afflictions. If you fail to train in this manner, the antidotes will not eliminate the adverse conditions, and you will fall prey to the afflictions, the master said.

The second method, vanquishing [the afflictions] through direct encounter, is this: Avoid acting like an elderly couple who are being robbed. Furthermore, when afflictions arise, they do not start out forcefully. They arise subtly at the beginning, so the moment they arise, you need to avert them by challenging them, thinking, "Who are you?" If you do this, you will not fall under their power; you will be able to overcome them through antidotes. If they are not averted at that point, their strength will increase, and they will then be difficult to overcome with antidotes. As if striking pig heads with a stick, drive afflictions away the moment they arise.

The third method, that of mocking, means to chide yourself for falling under the afflictions' power, thinking, "Alas! What kind of weakling are you? What point is there in such behavior?" Mock yourself in this way. Furthermore, when afflictions arise, think, "Because you behaved in this manner you are wandering in cyclic existence. Are you going to continue to behave like this?" Counter them and drive them away in this manner, the master said.

So for the preliminary, you conjure what is not there; for the actual practice, you vanquish through direct encounter; and for conclusion, you mock yourself, the master said.

The essential points of mind training are, the master said, (1) to heap together, (2) to generate, and (3) to purify. "To heap together" means, for example, contemplating during an illness, "There are unimaginable illnesses in the universe; may all of these befall me at this very moment, and may their continuum come to an end." In other words, you heap upon yourself the sufferings of all sentient beings.

"To generate" refers to visualizing a hollow light where you are and imagining that this increases in size, eventually swallowing everything into emptiness. You then place your mind naturally poised in this state, the master said.

"To purify" refers to visualizing a white *Āḥ*, which progressively diminishes and disappears, becoming devoid of intrinsic existence. You should then place your mind naturally poised in this state, the master said.

## 3. The purpose

There are four immediate virtues of Mahayana mind training, it has been taught: (1) It is the great counterbalance to happiness, (2) it is the great closure to your misery,[160] (3) it is the sympathetic friend if you live alone, and (4) it is the nurse when you are sick.

[*It is the great counterbalance to happiness.*] Without a teaching such as this mind training, then generally, you do not practice when things are going well; you develop an interest in practice only when your fortune declines. Recognize that since cyclic existence is in the nature of suffering, the perception that it is joyful is a delusion. When such a thought [that it is joyful] occurs, inquire, "Where does it arise from?" If it abides, ask, "Where does it abide?" If it ceases, analyze, "Where does it go when it ceases?" "What color and form does it have?" If you view [cyclic existence] in this manner, you will come to understand that it is devoid of intrinsic existence. This is the counterbalance to happiness.

[*It is the great closure to your misery.*] If you lack this type of spiritual practice, then when tragedy strikes, you tend to aggravate it with such thoughts as, "Why is this happening to me?" Whereas when you possess this mind training, usually you recognize self-grasping as the root cause of your suffering. The grasping at your body as "mine" is to blame. The coming together of the causes and conditions for suffering is to blame. Arrows cannot hit a target not put up; birds cannot land on a roof not erected. Similarly, if you do not grasp the body as "mine," you simply have no basis for suffering to arise. So your self-grasping is to blame. Without grasping as "mine" what you cherish so much in your heart, this situation will not arise. Can suffering exist in the earth, rocks, mountains, cliffs, or in empty space? As you probe in this manner, suffering is pacified. This is the closure to your misery.

*It is the sympathetic friend if you live alone.* Without a spiritual practice such as this, you cannot live alone [peacefully]. When indoors, you will feel like going out; when outside, you will feel like coming in. However, with a practice such as this, you recognize that, in general, self-grasping is the root cause of the suffering of all beings. So think, "Since grasping on to something as having intrinsic existence when in fact there is none makes me suffer, I will let go of it as best as I can. I will let go of it so that it is wiped clean."[161]

It is not true that the array of beings in cyclic existence are unconnected. Since all of them are your kind and dear parents, take their suffering into your heart and dedicate your happiness and virtues to them. As you practice by exchanging these two and even once experience its taste, days and nights will seem very short. So if you live alone, this mind training becomes a sympathetic friend.

*It is the nurse when you are sick.* If you lack this mind training, then when you become ill, no nurse will seem satisfactory. You will be plagued by such thoughts as "She could have done more for me, for she owes me a lot," and you will thus be consumed by thoughts about what others should have done for you. If on the other hand you possess this mind training, when you become ill, you will think like this: "No one is to blame for my illness; my own self-grasping is to blame. For without grasping on to self, sickness has no basis to arise. If I benefit from nursing, then I can recall how I have had nurses countless times in the past. There is no medicine I have not taken, no healing ritual that I have not had performed. As for treatment, there is no treatment I have not undergone. Whether I will become free from cyclic existence or not, today I will vanquish this self-grasping. Help me destroy it. I will derive great satisfaction [from destroying it]. I will vanquish this self-grasping and let it go."

Without annihilating this self-grasping, there is no attainment of buddhahood, the master said.

As you meditate with the thought, "It is my grasping at body as 'mine' that is to blame," your feeling of superiority to other beings will subside. This is how mind training acts as your nurse, the master said.

It has been taught that Mahayana mind training leads to the following way of being of one's body, speech, and mind:

> When suffering occurs, I will take on that of all beings;
> when virtue arises, I will dedicate it to all.
> Body and speech are like an illusion and an echo,
> while the clear-light mind is devoid of going and
>     coming.

The first [taking the sufferings of all beings] is twofold: taking them from what is nearest and taking them from what is greatest. Of these, the first is to contemplate with the thought, "May all the sufferings of my parents, friends, and relatives ripen upon me at this very instant. May the continuum of all these sufferings come to an end." The second is to contemplate with the thought, "May all the sufferings of the hell realms ripen upon me. May the continuum of all these sufferings come to an end." Then extend this to all beings and take their sufferings—from the hungry ghosts, from the animals, from the demigods, from the celestial gods, and from human beings.

To dedicate your virtues when virtues arise to the assembly of beings, whatever virtues arise, meditate with the thought, "May my roots of virtue come to fruition upon my two parents and upon all the sentient beings of the six classes. May all beings enjoy happiness and be free from suffering."

Regarding viewing your body and speech as illusions and echoes, the body is said to be like an illusion. Through the power of mantra and magical substances, the magician casts a spell on the eyes of the spectators, thus making them perceive various illusory creations, though he himself does not apprehend them as real. Even at the moment perceptions appear, things do not exist as such. Taking this mere appearance that transcends the extremes of both permanence and annihilation as a metaphor for the body, meditate on the absence of intrinsic existence in the face of appearances.

Likewise, speech is like an echo. For example, if you shout in a gorge with high cliffs, "O lady echo," you will receive exactly the same response. However, you cannot say that this exists [as speech], for it is an echo. Yet you cannot say that it does not exist either, for it is obviously there. With this illustration of mere appearance, meditate on how speech is indistinguishable from an echo and, in this manner, meditate on the absence of intrinsic existence.

"The clear-light mind is devoid of going and coming" indicates that for this mind of clear light, you cannot say that it has gone somewhere, nor can you say that it abides somewhere. Devoid of origination, cessation, and abiding, and not existing with any identity, it is like space.

So the body is like an illusion, speech is like an echo, and the mind is devoid of intrinsic existence. Place your mind naturally poised in this state of absence of intrinsic existence, the master said.

May this instruction stemming from the glorious [Atiśa] Dīpaṃkara remain ever excellent!

# Formal Practices

The last two texts can be seen as presenting complete formal mind training sitting meditations, one a "reviewing meditation" (*shargom*) of the key points of Atiśa's *Root Lines on Mind Training*, the other a distinct formal meditative cultivation of compassion.

*Mind Training in a Single Session*, by the famed master of Sangphu Monastery Chim Namkha Drak (1210–85), is a beautiful example of how the central themes of mind training teachings can be meditated upon within a single session. This work is actually designed for use in a daily sitting practice, so that meditators can reinforce their practical application of mind training principles through their formal meditative endeavor.

The author of this short formal meditation, Chim Namkha Drak, was the seventh abbot of Narthang Monastery, one of the most important learning centers associated with the Kadam school. Among his teachers of mind training include Sangyé Gompa, the author of the lengthy *Public Explication of Mind Training* (translated in *Mind Training: The Great Collection*). Chim also wrote what later became the "standard" biography of Master Atiśa. Because of his repute, both as an authority on classical Buddhist thought as well as a master of meditative instructions, especially of mind training, he came to be highly revered across the various Tibetan traditions and acquired the epithet the All-Knowing Chim (*Chim thamché khyenpa*).

*Glorious Virvapa's Mind Training* presents a special instruction on the meditative cultivation of universal compassion from the Indian adept Virvapa. The text cites first an eight-line quotation and later a six-line quote from Virvapa, which form the "root text" for this work. The practice of compassion presented here consists of two distinct yogas. The first is a unique approach called "the unparalleled yoga of compassion," a practice that involves focusing specially on an adversary. This is followed by meditation on *tonglen*, or giving and taking, which the text calls "the yoga of root cause." The instruction concludes with a meditation on the empty and illusion-like nature of all things.

Though attributed to Lo Lotsāwa, the source of the mind training instruction presented here is identified in its "colophon" as one Darpaṇa Ācārya, who, in turn, was presenting the thought of the Indian mystic Virvapa. If, as some Tibetan commentators suggest, Virvapa is the same person as Virūpa, the author of the root text of the Sakya Lamdré cycle of teaching, *Vajra Lines on the Path and Its Fruits*, our original author can be then placed sometime in the eighth century, for Virūpa is generally recognized to be the same person as the Indian Nālandā master Dharmapāla.

Lo Lotsāwa Sherap Rinchen was a Tibetan translator born sometime in the latter part of the twelfth century. He traveled to Nepal and India and received extensive teachings from many Indian masters and was also a student of the great Sakya Paṇḍita. Intriguingly, neither Darpaṇa Ācārya nor the Tibetan *lotsāwa* appear in the lineage of instruction given in the colophon. The final "me" in the colophon is Könchog Gyaltsen, second abbot of Ngor Monastery and one of the compilers of *Mind Training: The Great Collection.*

# 17. Mind Training in a Single Session
### *Chim Namkha Drak*

Homage to the teachers, the perfect spiritual friends!

THERE ARE THREE POINTS to this instruction: [(1) the preparatory practice, (2) the main practice, and (3) the concluding practice.]

## 1. The preparatory practice

The first, the preparatory practice, is as follows. In a solitary place, a site free of conditions not conducive to observing pure ethical conduct, sit on a comfortable cushion and then go for refuge and generate the awakening mind. Then contemplate your body as devoid of substantial reality, like a balloon filled with air. Imagine your heart as a mass of white light, and at your crown visualize your root teacher seated on a moon cushion upon a lotus, and contemplate him to be the sole embodiment of all the lineage masters from the Buddha to the present, of the teachers from whom you have actually received teachings, of the meditation deities, and of all the buddhas and bodhisattvas. Prostrate to them mentally and make offerings to them.

The supplication is this:

> O my gurus, you who are perfect spiritual friends, please attend to me.

> Bless me, O my gurus, you who are perfect spiritual
> friends, so that unblemished realizations of Mahayana
> mind training may arise within me.
> Bless me so that I may subdue the grasping at "I"
> and "self" this very instant and that I may understand
> all adversities and obstacles as aids to Dharma
> practice.

Make this supplication three times.

While imagining "My mind is an actual buddha who has eliminated all defects, including their propensities, and who is endowed with every higher quality," take refuge in the body, speech, and mind of your teacher. Then imagine that your teacher descends through your crown aperture and enters your heart, which is a mass of light, and contemplate that this is an actual buddha. As your teacher's body, speech, and mind dissolve into you, they become the ultimate expanse (*dharmadhātu*), which is the great clear light. Leave your mind in this state for as long as it abides. When thoughts arise, visualize your teacher at your crown, make dedications toward the fulfillment of his enlightened aspirations, and supplicate him. Engage in this meditation approximately six times during day and night, and so on. Then whatever meditative absorptions you aspire to will arise in your mental continuum.

**First, train in the preliminaries.**

This is threefold: (1) As for the rarity of attaining a human existence of leisure and opportunity, contemplate the qualities of leisure and opportunity and take their essence. Since mind training is the supreme Dharma practice, you should engage in it. (2) Even if you obtain a human life of leisure and opportunity, you cannot live forever, and you could die at any time if the force of your karma is exhausted. At the time of death, there is no worse tragedy than dying with remorse, bereft of any Dharma realization. Therefore train your mind. (3) After death you do not stop becoming; you must take rebirth. Wherever you may be reborn in cyclic existence will be subject to suffering. Therefore relinquish cyclic existence, and to this end, practice mind training. Purify your mental continuum of negative karma and the obstructions you have accumulated, and toward others cultivate loving-kindness, compassion, and the awakening mind.

## 2. The main practice

The main practice has two parts, of which the first, the conventional awakening mind, is as follows.

> **Train alternately in the two—giving and taking.**
> **Commence the sequence of taking from your own self.**

Imagine that all the sufferings and their causes that are likely to befall you in your future lives, including even those that might materialize tomorrow, bear fruit at this very instant. Reflecting in this way has the advantage of transforming adverse conditions into favorable ones. Then cultivate loving-kindness and compassion toward your real-life mother and, from the depths of your heart, take all her sufferings and their causes upon yourself. Similarly, take the subtle obscuration to knowledge from all sentient beings and the three noble beings.[162] In brief, you take upon your heart all the deficiencies of samsara and nirvana from all beings except your teachers and the buddhas. Taking these repeatedly, when your shoulders ache, imagine your body to be a balloon filling with air that expands to pervade the entirety of space. Then place your mind in the absence of intrinsic existence.

As you meditate on emptiness, reflect, "How sad that all these mothers of mine are caught within the immediate conditions of suffering and cyclic existence. I will free them from these immediate conditions of suffering and place them in unsurpassed bliss and happiness, and to this end I will give away everything—my body, wealth, and roots of virtue." Thinking in this manner, transform your body into a precious wish-fulfilling jewel and confer, to all your dear mothers, material resources equal to the wealth of all gods and humans filling all of space, as well as your virtues accumulated throughout the three times. As you give these, imagine that your mothers enjoy the perfect gathering of all favorable conditions for Dharma practice and that they accomplish the two accumulations and attain perfect buddhahood. Make this contemplation in regard to all sentient beings.

**Place the two astride your breath.**

This indicates that when you exhale, you give all your wealth and virtues to sentient beings, and as you practice in this manner and experience the dawning of meditative concentration, you then take on the sufferings and their causes of both yourself and others. When you engage in this way, it is said, you derive the benefit of attaining the realization of mind training as these meditative absorptions arise within you.

Second, the meditation on the ultimate awakening mind is as follows:

**Having become trained, engage in the secret point.**[163]

This suggests that when you are able to exchange your virtues with others' sufferings, you then meditate on emptiness, which is kept secret from the weak-minded. This is as follows:

All phenomena are in general subsumed into the two classes of object and subject. As you then examine individually all the objects that appear as material realities, they are reduced to subtle particles. Invariably, these turn out to be midpoints interfacing the six directions,[164] which means they are not established as substantially real singular entities. And since they do not exist as substantially real multiple entities either, meditate on the nonsubstantiality of materially constituted realities.

As for inner awareness, the past is no more, the future is yet to be, and the present is devoid of color, shape, and spatial location. If it does not exist in such a manner, then it does not exist as a substantial reality. Therefore, contemplate inner awareness too as devoid of substantially real existence.

Since the external world of material realities does not exist, then the object of meditation does not exist; and since what appears as inner awareness also does not exist, then the meditating mind too does not exist. This freedom from the object of meditation and the meditating mind is called "exhausting knowable objects," and to abide unwavering in this state is "to meditate on suchness." As such, just as the objective world does not exist in any mode, the mind too does not grasp it in any way. So place your mind naturally with ease in the state of nonconceptuality. It has been taught:

> A mind entangled in knots,
> if undone, will no doubt be free.[165]

When all acts of dissipation and withdrawal of conceptualization cease, this is "tranquil abiding"; and when the mind remains clear and lucid while free of conceptualization, with no grasping at any signs, this is referred to as "penetrative insight."

Initially, you should meditate in many short sessions, and when you have gained stability, you can remain there as long as your mind stays focused. When you wish to rise, cultivate compassion toward all sentient beings and then dedicate the merit. During the actual meditation, alternate the practice of the conventional and ultimate awakening minds. As your familiarity grows, even if you cannot accomplish everything, you can engage in the practice of giving and taking at the level of mere illusion-like conventional reality, free of [belief in] substantial reality and clinging.

## 3. The concluding practice

"**Three objects, three poisons**" indicates that it is in relation to the three objects that the three poisons come into being, and you should transform these into the "**three roots of virtue.**" For example, when you experience attachment toward attractive forms, which are objects of your eyes, you take into the core of your heart the attachments of other sentient beings. Imagine that as you give your body, wealth, and roots of virtue to all sentient beings, all beings come to possess the root virtue of nonattachment. Toward visual forms you dislike, imagine that you are free of aversion, and contemplate in a similar manner toward the objects of your ignorance. Likewise, contemplate in the same manner when each of the three poisons arises with respect to whatever occurs—sounds to the ear, odors to the nose, tastes to the tongue, and tactile sensations to the body.

**In all actions, train by means of the words.**

This suggests that during all your everyday activities—standing, sitting, or sleeping—you recite whatever is most appropriate, such as "May the sufferings and their origins of all beings ripen upon me this very instant. May the 'self' suffer downfall; may the 'self' and 'real entities' become no more and be lost forever.

May my body, wealth, and roots of virtue ripen upon sentient beings. May sentient beings attain all higher qualities of the path and the results of these this very instant." Your actions will then follow after your speech, and, it is said, the benefit of [these realizations] will then arise swiftly in your mind.

This work entitled *Mind Training in a Single Session* was composed by the abbot of Narthang, the great Chim Namkha Drak. May its excellence equal space!

# 18. Glorious Virvapa's Mind Training
## Lo Lotsāwa

Homage to the teachers!

THE GLORIOUS VIRVAPA said:

> To those who've nurtured you with affection,
> these embodiments of kindness, contemplate them with
> compassion.
> "This agent of harm, too, is my mother!
> Though she has shown me kindness repeatedly in the
> past,
> like an insane person, she today has no self-control.
> Owing to her negative karma, she is suffering in the hell
> of Avīci."

> As you contemplate thus, you perfect
> your compassion for all three realms of existence.

## 1. The yoga of unparalleled compassion

Compassion is the root of Mahayana teachings. If this is absent, regardless of whatever aspects of the path you might have—such as the six perfections and the generation and completion stages of your solemn pledges—you will fall into the ranks of the Lesser Vehicle. You need, therefore, to possess loving-kindness, compassion, and the awakening mind. Loving-kindness brings benefits, while compassion is cultivated by starting with those who harm you.

So, in a secluded place, adopt a balanced physical lifestyle; take refuge [in the Three Jewels] and generate the awakening mind. Imagine yourself as a meditation deity and visualize your teacher at the crown of your head. Then visualize in front of you an enemy who causes serious harm to you and to others. Then engage in the meditative practice of compassion by combining both its continuum and its rationale.[166]

First, while maintaining a vigilant posture, focus your mind single-pointedly on your enemy. Then verbally recite the following a hundred, fifty, or twenty-one times, as if it were an incantation: "Pitiable indeed is this enemy who causes me harm." This is the meditation on the continuum.

The second [the meditation on its rationale] is as follows: (1) Reflecting, "This enemy is bound to have been my mother in the past. Ah, my poor mother!" cultivate compassion toward her repeatedly.[167]

(2) Why should you have compassion for her? "She has been my mother not just once or twice, but many times." Reflecting thus, develop compassion toward her repeatedly.

(3) Why should you have compassion for her? "Every time she was my mother, she showed me immeasurable kindness." Reflecting thus, develop compassion repeatedly.

(4) Why should you have compassion for her? "Mothers generally do only beneficial things, so why is this enemy causing harm? Although this enemy is indeed my mother, she has not mastered her consciousness and today is like an insane person. How sad! Not only does she harm other sentient beings, but she harms her own child as well!" Reflecting thus, develop compassion for her repeatedly.

(5) Why should you have compassion for her? "Due to her

harmful actions, she will be reborn in the hell of Avīci and will be oppressed by intense suffering. Ah, my poor mother, this agent of harm!" Repeat this many times.

As you meditate in this way—combining the object, incantations, and the five rationales for developing compassion— you generate compassion in full accordance with the appearance of the following signs: Tears flow from your eyes, your hairs stand on end, the energy of your body and mind become tireless, and so on. Reflecting, "I will attain buddhahood for the benefit of all beings, especially the agents of harm," generate the awakening mind and imagine that all sentient beings, including those who harm you, attain the state of meditation deities. Place your mind for a long period in this wisdom free of conceptual elaboration. When conceptualization begins, perform the dedication.

When you have developed compassion toward one in this way, then extend it to others, such as medium and lesser agents of harm. Then extend it to your relatives, your fellow Tibetans, the people the earth, the four continents, and the trichilicosmic worlds, pervading the expanse of space. Your compassion will then become infinite. Because of this, your hatred and anger will naturally diminish; and such difficulties as leprosy and demon possessions will subside naturally of their own accord. Your mind will transform into affection for all beings, like a mother's love for her only child. The extraordinary wisdom that is free of conceptual elaboration will arise as well.

## 2. The yoga of root cause

[Virvapa] said:

> Assailed by inner and outer elaborations,
> when your awareness is in turmoil,

recall this awakening mind
that exchanges self and others.
This will destroy the army of afflictions and māras
and transform them into wisdom free of elaboration.

As stated here, the awakening mind is the cause for attaining the state of omniscience. This is twofold—the conventional and ultimate awakening minds—of which the ultimate is the wisdom free of conceptual elaboration. Although the first, conventional awakening mind, has various forms, here we focus on the practice taught by our teacher of exchanging self and others, which is as follows:

When you are plagued by grave physical illness or a sorrowful heart, both of which are suffering, when you are assailed by enemies, demon possessions, or an imbalance of natural elements, or when forceful afflictions arise in you, take all these as ingredients of your path. For instance, when strong aversion arises, think, "Through the arising of this aversion may all the instances of aversion and its causes existing in the hearts of hostile beings ripen upon me."

Also aspire, "May all the sufferings—which are the fruits of afflictions and are rooted in self-grasping—existing in the minds of sentient beings manifest upon me. In particular, may the specific sufferings—such as the experiences of being burned, inflamed, and so on of the hell beings; the hunger and thirst of the hungry ghosts; the killing and servitude of the animals; the quarrels and conflicts of the demigods; the human sufferings of birth, aging, sickness, and death, plus the illnesses of the sick, the poverty and deprivation of the poor, and the suffering of having defective organs—ripen upon my own suffering. May all the obstacles and conditions that obstruct my attainments—from a human existence of leisure and opportunity to the realization of the grounds and paths—mature upon this aversion of mine."

In this way, concentrate your entire body, speech, and mind, and single-pointedly collect the sufferings of all sentient beings upon yourself. Meditate in this way for one, two, or three hours and so on while maintaining single-pointed focus. Meditate until the conceptual processes, such as the afflictions, are pacified. Turn these into aspects of your path until the suffering of illness ceases. Recite aloud, "May the sufferings of all beings fall upon me."[168]

Then visualize that all your virtues—both their causes and their fruits—such as your two accumulations, emanate from your heart like the rays of a rising sun. Imagine that they touch the sentient beings, who are then led to the state of meditation deities, the nature of Buddha's body and wisdom. As you then place your mind in the wisdom free of conceptual elaboration, an extraordinary wisdom dawns within. When conceptualization reappears, perform the dedication.

Those on the beginner's level should practice in this manner. Once you gain greater familiarity, then whatever thoughts arise—gross or subtle conceptual processes, fear, suffering, and so on—assimilate them as before and focus on them single-pointedly. Recite aloud, "Through my virtues, may all beings attain happiness."[169]

Imagine that your body, wealth, and positive karma ripen upon sentient beings and that they thus attain uncontaminated bliss. The difference here lies in the pace of the visualization. With respect to purpose, there is no difference [between beginning meditators and experienced ones]. As for the concluding practice, it is the same as the previous one [that is, to perform the dedication when conceptualization recurs].

The immediate benefits of the conventional awakening mind are that thought processes such as the afflictions subside, you gain release from sickness and demon possessions, you become beneficial to all beings, and you bring them under your sphere of influence. Ultimately, you attain the states of a buddha's enjoyment body and emanation body and thus bring about the perfect welfare of others. Through the ultimate awakening mind you achieve the seed of dharmakāya and thus attain the great seal (*mahāmudrā*), which is the supreme attainment.

When such auspicious conditions are gathered, all kinds of signs associated with your body, speech, and mind emerge. In particular the mental states free of subject-object duality— tranquil abiding and penetrative insight—arise in your mental continuum. You then abide in what is known as *the singular instance of reflexive awareness*, which is an instance of cognition that embodies the five wisdoms: The empty, nonconceptual mind is dharma body; the self-cognition is the enjoyment body; while its luminosity is the emanation body. The indivisibility of these three is the self-nature body. (1) Since the mind itself is free from all conceptual elaborations, it is the wisdom of the ultimate expanse; (2) its cognition of itself as empty is the mirrorlike wisdom; (3) its self-cognition is the discriminative awareness; (4) its illumination of itself is the wisdom accomplishing all deeds; and (5) their indivisibility is the wisdom of equanimity.

## Colophon

The lineage of the transmission of this guide by Lo Lotsāwa on the instruction of unparalleled compassion—the intention of the glorious Virvapa and the teaching of Darpaṇa Ācārya—is as follows: Vajradhāra, Virvapa, Jetsün Ḍombipa, Jetsün Mathipa, the siddha Ṇikalava, Jetsün Ravaintapa, Chak Lotsāwa Chöjé Pal, Lama Dampa Shönu Gyaltsen, Vajradhāra Matiśrī, Lama Yeshé Shap, Sangpoi Pal. He passed the lineage to Buddharatna, he to Kīrtiśīla, he to Jayabhadra, he to Puṇyaratna, he to Shönu Gyalchok, and he to me.

Through whatever pure virtue may stem from this,
may all sentient beings residing in the cycle of existence
attain the pure thought of emptiness and compassion,
and be led swiftly to the state of stainless bliss.

# Notes

1  This introduction is adapted and expanded from my introduction to *Mind Training: The Great Collection* (Boston: Wisdom Publications, 2006) to suit a wider readership. Those interested in more detailed understanding of the origins and development of the mind training instructions, as well as the diverse lineage of instructions on the famed *Seven-Point Mind Training*, please consult my introduction to that earlier volume as well as my annotations to the earliest commentary on the *Seven-Point* there.

2  The Dalai Lama's lecture in Central Park can be found in *Open Heart* (New York: Little, Brown, 2002). Another commentary by the Dalai Lama on *Eight Verses* can be found in *The Compassionate Life* (Boston: Wisdom Publications, 2003).

3  For a clear and succinct explanation of the theoretical understanding of the process of such transformation of the mind and its basis, see H. H. the Dalai Lama, *Transforming the Mind*, trans. by Thupten Jinpa (London: Thorsons, 2000), pp. 1–19.

4  A lucid translation of this important Buddhist classic in English exists under the title *Bodhicaryāvatāra* in the Oxford World's Classics series (New York: Oxford University Press, 1995). This translation, undertaken by Andrew Skilton and Kate Crosby, was based on the extant Sanskrit version with comparison to the canonical Tibetan edition of the work. The translation also contains succinct summary of the key points at the beginning of each chapter, thus helping the modern reader become familiar with the structure of the individual chapters. The meditations on equalizing and exchanging of self and others are found in chapter 8 of this Buddhist classic.

5  A simple internet search on "mind training" or "Seven-Point Mind Training" yields numerous English translations of these root texts and also contemporary renderings of their lines in the form of spiritual slogans.

6  Thupten Jinpa, trans., *Mind Training: The Great Collection*, pp. 57–70.

7  *Mind Training: The Great Collection*, p. 317. Ostensibly composed as an epistle to an Indian king, Nāgārjuna's (second century) *Precious Garland* presents the entire Mahayana path to full enlightenment. Sharawa refers specifically to the lines "May their negative karma ripen upon me. / May all my virtues ripen upon them." (5:84cd) as a source of the mind training instruction on taking on others' suffering and offering one's own happiness to others.

8  As interest in understanding the more positive qualities of the human mind grows, truly secular programs for systematic training in compassion are being developed. I have personally been involved in the development of such a program at Stanford University entitled CCT (Compassion Cultivation Training).

9  Chapter 12 of the present volume is an exposition of Śākyaśrī's mind training instruction as encapsulated in these four lines.

10  Quoted in Sangyé Gompa's *Public Explication of Mind Training* (in *Mind Training: The Great Collection*, p. 399).

11  *Dze chos. Mind Training: The Great Collection*, p. 318.

12  For a critical examination of the role of Dharmarakṣita as Atiśa's teacher, especially on the awakening mind, see the introduction by Michael Sweet and Leonard Zwilling in Geshe Lhundub Sopa et al., *Peacock in the Poison Grove* (Boston: Wisdom Publications, 1996), pp. 4–8.

13  There are several "biographies" of Atiśa, the most well known being the *Source of Teachings*, which is attributed to Dromtönpa, as well as the *Extensive Biography* and the *Standard Biography* of Chim Namkha Drak. For a critical analysis of the tradition of Atiśa's biographies, see Helmut Eimer, "The Development of the Biographical Tradition Concerning Atiśa (Dīpaṃkaraśrījñāna)," *The Journal of the Tibet Society, London* 2 (1982): 41–51.

14  Shönu Gyalchok, one of the two compilers of *Mind Training: The Great Collection*, also writes that the *Seven-Point Mind Training* "is drawn from those composed by Atiśa with minor modifications of wording to help make them easier to understand. This is not an independently authored work." Shönu Gyalchok, *Mind Training: Compendium of Well-Uttered Insights* (Delhi: Ngawang Topgyal, 1996), p. 96b. That the tradition of compiling the miscellaneous instructions of the Kadam masters existed very early in the history of the Kadam school is evidenced from the well-known *Miscellaneous Sayings of the*

*Kadam Masters*, compiled and edited by Chegom Sherap Dorjé (twelfth century), an English translation of which can be found in Thupten Jinpa, trans., *The Book of Kadam: The Core Texts*, The Library of Tibetan Classics 2 (Boston: Wisdom Publications, 2007), pp. 559–610.

15 Due to the divergences among the various redactions of the *Seven-Point Mind Training*, a student of Phabongkha Dechen Nyingpo (1878–1941) requested that he produce a "critical" edition. Comparing the various extant redactions and on the basis of consultation with numerous commentaries, Phabongkha produced a version that is consonant with the approach of Tsongkhapa. A translation of this appears as an appendix to Phabongkha's *Liberation in the Palm of Your Hand*, trans. by Michael Richards (Boston: Wisdom Publications, 2006), pp. 726–30.

16 On the whole, the Geluk authors use the root text embedded in Hortön Namkha Pal's *Rays of the Sun*, which accords with the tradition of Sangyé Gompa, while most non-Geluk authors use the root text embedded in Thokmé Sangpo's commentary. In this latter text, the training in the ultimate awakening mind comes earlier.

17 For a translation of the core of this *Book of Kadam* as well as an account of the emergence of the teachings contained in it, see Thupten Jinpa, trans., *The Book of Kadam*.

18 "Faith" here refers to a profound faith in the law of karma.

19 The Tibetan term *khenpo*, translated here as "preceptor," can also mean an abbot of a monastery. Here the term refers to spiritual masters who have conferred vows and precepts upon you.

20 "Both" here refers to the two ends of the spectrum of one's fluctuating state, namely, self-importance (which arises when one's state of mind is overly excited) and discouragement (which arises when one's state of mind becomes too deflated).

21 The ten spiritual deeds or Dharma-related activities, are (1) inscribing the words of scripture, (2) making offerings to the buddhas and bodhisattvas, (3) giving charity, (4) listening to the Dharma, (5) upholding it, (6) reading it, (7) expounding it, (8) reciting it on a daily basis, (9) contemplating the meaning of the Dharma, (10) and meditating on its meaning.

22 The seven limbs are a set of practices that developed in the Mahayana tradition based on canonical sources. The seven are (1) performing prostrations, (2) making offerings, (3) declaring and

purifying nonvirtue, (4) rejoicing in your own and others' virtuous deeds, (5) appealing to the enlightened ones not to enter into nirvana, (6) supplicating the enlightened beings to turn the wheel of Dharma, and finally (7) dedicating all your virtues to the attainment of enlightenment for the benefit of all beings.

23   The two defilements are the two kinds of obscurations—the obscurations of the afflictions, which obstruct liberation, and the subtle obscurations to omniscience, which prevent buddhahood.

24   The Tibetan original uses the instrumental case after the "two," giving the following reading: "Be upheld principally by the two witnesses." However, we have chosen here to follow the more established reading, according to which we are advised to uphold our own self, rather than some other person, to be the most important witness to our thoughts and actions.

25   Serlingpa's personal name is Dharmakīrti, which literally means "renowned in the Dharma."

26   "Mantra" here refers to the entire system of Buddhist thought and practice known as Vajrayana, while "Perfection" refers to the general Mahayana tradition known as the sutra or "perfection" system.

27   The six parameters are part of a unique interpretive method that sets the conditions within which a correct reading of a Vajrayana text of the highest yoga class must take place. The six parameters consist of three sets of contrasts—provisional versus definitive, literal versus nonliteral, and finally that which has an implicit intent versus that which does not.

28   Tib. *Dbyug pa gsum gyi phreng ba*. This sutra does not appear to have been translated into Tibetan.

29   *Sūtrālaṃkāra*. There is no such entry under Aśvaghoṣa's name in the Tengyur. However a Chinese translation of the text exists under the title *Kie man louen*.

30   This is Asaṅga's (ca. fourth century) text entitled *Bodhisattvabhūmi*.

31   *Vimalakīrtinirdeśasūtra*, chap. 7, 215a5. "Perishable composite" refers to the collection of the five aggregates—form, feeling, discrimination, mental formations, and consciousness—that together make up the existence of a person. Classical Buddhist texts often refer to the view of a self as the *view of the perishable composite*.

32   The three Kadam brothers are Potowa, Chengawa, and Puchungwa, who were principal disciples of Master Dromtönpa and later became the chief custodians of the three principal lineages of Kadam teachings.

33 This is a reference to Dromtönpa, who founded the famous Kadam monastery of Radreng, a site famed for juniper trees.

34 The "three scopes" are the framework within which Atiśa famously organized the teaching of the path to enlightenment in his seminal *Lamp for the Path to Enlightenment*. The term *scope* relates to the capacity or the level of the aspirant, with the initial scope, or capacity, defined in terms of someone whose primary spiritual goal is to attain freedom from the fears of unfortunate rebirth. Persons of medium scope are those aspirants whose primary spiritual goal is freedom from unenlightened cyclic existence, or *samsara*. In contrast, the persons of great scope are those aspirants who seek full enlightenment for the benefit all beings. For a concise exposition of Atiśa's *Lamp*, see chapter 3 of the Dalai Lama's *Lighting the Way* (Ithaca, NY: Snow Lion Publications, 2004).

35 Literally, "chamber of divinities" (*lhai khangpa*; spelled *lha'i khang pa*), where the practitioner would have images of revered beings, such as the Buddha, installed on the altar. The abbreviated form of this word, *lhakhang*, is often translated in English as "temple."

36 "Master" here refers to Chekawa, Sé Chilbu's teacher.

37 The "basis-of-all," or *kunshi*, is a technical term that is the translation of the Sanskrit word *ālaya*, a term that has close association with the notion of store consciousness (*ālayavijñāna*) of the Mind Only school. In the context of the *Seven-Point Mind Training*, the term is explained differently by different authors, some taking it to refer to an uncontrived natural state of the mind, others taking it to refer to emptiness, the ultimate nature of reality.

38 On the seven limbs, see note 22.

39 *A Guide to the Bodhisattva's Way of Life* 8:120, 28a5.

40 *A Guide to the Bodhisattva's Way of Life* 8:131, 28b4.

41 *A Guide to the Bodhisattva's Way of Life* 8:136, 28b7.

42 The metaphor implied here is that of grabbing a dog by its snout.

43 Śāntideva, *A Guide to the Bodhisattva's Way of Life* 5:70, 13a1.

44 The "great lord of the ten levels" is the Buddha, who has perfected all ten bodhisattva levels (*bhūmi*) of purification and development.

45 The "five poisons" of the mind are the afflictions of attachment, anger, delusion, pride, and jealousy.

46 Bhūripa's *Extensive Daily Confessions of Cakrasaṃvara Practice*, 95a4.

47 The "four everyday activities" are the four physical activities a monk typically engages in on a daily basis: traveling, strolling, lying down, and sitting.

48  Dharmakīrti, *Thorough Exposition of Valid Cognition* 2:221, 116a1.

49  Śāntideva, *A Guide to the Bodhisattva's Way of Life* 8:113, 28a1.

50  Śāntideva, *A Guide to the Bodhisattva's Way of Life* 8:155, 29b3.

51  In Tibetan society this facial expression conveys determination and courage in the face of an enemy's challenge. Warriors from the Gesar epic are often depicted with this expression during battle.

52  *A Guide to the Bodhisattva's Way of Life* 4:34, 9a7. The last line differs slightly from the version in the Dergé canon.

53  This is probably an old Tibetan saying. A slightly different version of this saying reads: "Living on the head yet throwing mud into the eyes." The saying describes the ingratitude of someone who deliberately harms those from whom he or she has received benefits.

54  *A Guide to the Bodhisattva's Way of Life* 8:129–30, 28b3.

55  In Tibetan folk belief, the hooting of owls is considered a bad omen, an intimation of misfortune to come, such as the death of a loved one.

56  *A Guide to the Bodhisattva's Way of Life* 8:154, 29b:3.

57  Śāntideva, *A Guide to the Bodhisattva's Way of Life* 8:169, 30a4.

58  I have failed to locate the source of this enumeration system. The classification of afflictions into six root and twenty derivative ones is found in Vasubandhu's (ca. fourth century) classic *Treasury of Higher Knowledge* (*Abhidharmakośa*).

59  *A Guide to the Bodhisattva's Way of Life* 8:121, 28a5. I have followed the canonical reading of the first line here.

60  Shawo Gangpa was a student of the famous Kadam master Gönpawa Wangchuk Gyaltsen (1016–82), who was, in turn, a prominent student of both Atiśa and Dromtönpa.

61  The spiritual mentor Ben refers to Ben Gungyal, a student of the Kadam master Gönpawa. This saying is one of the most well known by him that is cited in many other Tibetan texts.

62  This metaphor is found in Nāgārjuna's *Friendly Letter* 69cd, 43b7. Lokesh Chandra provides *kolāsita* as the Sanskrit equivalent of the Tibetan word *rgya shug gi tshig gu*. Since I have failed to identify what this tree is supposed to be, I have left its Sanskrit name in my translation here.

63  *Condensed Perfection of Wisdom in Stanzas*, 12b6. "Elemental spirits" are nonhuman agents, sometimes thought to cause energy imbalances and illness, according to ancient Indian and Tibetan medical systems.

64  The Tibetan word *dzené* (*dze nad*), which is often translated as "leprosy," might also be referring to another highly contagious skin disease.

This illness appears to have been a major health concern during the time of the early Kadam teachers in the eleventh and twelfth centuries in the central and southern regions of Tibet.

65  Śāntideva, *A Guide to the Bodhisattva's Way of Life* 3:12abd and 13d, 7a3.

66  The first two lines of this stanza do not appear in Atiśa's *Root Lines* and are also absent in many subsequent editions of the *Seven-Point Mind Training*.

67  *Vajra Peak Tantra*, 205b2.

68  In other words, like these impossible phenomena, one's obstructions are baseless.

69  I have failed to discern what list this is.

70  Śāntideva, *A Guide to the Bodhisattva's Way of Life* 6:21b, 15a7.

71  Śāntideva, *A Guide to the Bodhisattva's Way of Life* 6:21c, 15a7.

72  The "four powers" are basic elements common to all practices for purifying negative actions: the generation of a sincere regret, reliance on the Three Jewels, the performance of the ritual, and the resolve to not repeat the action.

73  The Tibetan text of this saying from Langri Thangpa is somewhat oblique. What it seems to be stating is that, without the prior cessation of bondage to hopes and fears, simply training in differentiating between friends and enemies and relating to others as friends would be too difficult, analogous to straightening a crooked tree.

74  On the ten spiritual activities, see note 21.

75  Readers will notice that the order of the five powers in this section is different from the one presented immediately before. While the former presents the standard sequence of the five powers, here the sequence is that of transferring consciousness at the time of death.

76  "Gifts of the deceased" (*spong thag*), literally, the "mark of renunciation," are articles belonging to a deceased person that are offered to a lama or a monastery, or sometimes to the poor, when requests for the performance of the death ritual are made. It became customary in Tibet, especially for dedicated religious practitioners, to make such offerings even before death. This is to encourage acceptance of the reality of your death so that you can let go of attachment to your possessions and concentrate on meditative practice, such as mind training, with increased urgency.

77  The meaning of this sentence is obscure. It may be an allusion to a Tibetan "death deception" (*'chi bslu*) ritual, where a dough likeness of a

sick person is outfitted with make-believe possessions, including, among other things, cloth from the person's clothes. If this interpretation is correct, the author is here underlining that the offerings being made to "embodiments of kindness," namely one's spiritual teachers, monastic community, and so on, should be real possessions, not facsimiles.

78  That is, the mind's ultimate nature, emptiness, is not subject to transference at the time of death.

79  This peculiar expression indicates a visceral strength of single-pointed perseverance in spiritual practice.

80  These are two contrasting sets of four things that are often the source of much of our emotional reaction of joy and pain: (1) receiving gifts, (2) fame, (3) praise, and (4) pleasure versus (1) receiving nothing, (2) disrepute, (3) criticism, and (4) pain. Reacting to one set with joy and the other with distress is characterized in the Buddhist texts as being under the power of "eight worldly concerns."

81  A harmful tree brings misfortune to one who chops it down. All the behaviors listed here are, in one way or another, considered risky and transgressive. The point is that the practitioner of mind training should not flaunt his or her courage and sense of invincibility.

82  Atiśa, *Bodhisattva's Jewel Garland*, stanzas 17c and 13d respectively; see chapter 1 of the present volume.

83  Nāgārjuna, *Precious Garland* 3:74, 117a5.

84  The commentary does not make explicit the correlation between the two methods of applying antidotes—investigation and close analysis—and the present and future afflictions. It is clear, however, that "investigation"—discerning the affliction most dominant in your mind and striving to diminish its force—relates to present afflictions, and "close analysis"—the detailed casual analysis of the afflictions upon which you strive to prevent their arising in the first place—relates to future afflictions.

85  The English word *boastfulness* does not fully convey the Tibetan word *yü* (*yud*). *Yü*, strongly abhorred in Tibetan culture, refers to deliberate, excessive expectation of recognition for some beneficial or kind act one has performed. It might involve constantly reminding others of the act done, or certain attitudes or bodily expressions that draw attention to it. Since *yü* comes from craving recognition, it involves self-cherishing, which is a key target of attack for the practitioner of mind

training. There is a well-known Tibetan saying: "For he who boasts of
his acts, no recognition is due" (*las byas yud can la byas ngo med*).

86 Radrengpa here refers to Dromtönpa, the principal student of Atiśa
and founder of Radreng Monastery near Lhasa.

87 Chakshingwa was a principal student of Gya Chakriwa, who was in
turn an important student of Langri Thangpa. This would place
Chakshingwa sometime in the early part of the twelfth century.

88 *A Guide to the Bodhisattva's Way of Life* 4:17, 8b5.

89 This story appears in *Mind Training: The Great Collection* as chapter
31, "The Story of the Repulsive Mendicant." The story tells of an ugly
mendicant who was hanging around a tavern somewhere in central
India when the local Buddhist monastery needed someone to rebuff
the constant challenges to debate from non-Buddhist scholars. The
monks learned from the local tavern lady of this odd-looking mendicant, who always uttered a strange word whenever she threw leftover
beer at him. This mendicant turned out to be highly learned, and he
helped the monastery to rise to the debate challenge.

90 *Condensed Perfection of Wisdom in Stanzas*, 19a6.

91 Maitreya, *Ornament of Mahayana Sutras* 10:81cd, 12a4. The Tengyur
reads slightly differently.

92 Walking toward a destination, going for a stroll, sleeping, and sitting—these are referred to as the four everyday activities in the earliest
Buddhist scriptures, especially those that relate to the monastic vows.

93 *A Guide to the Bodhisattva's Way of Life* 4:44, 9b7.

94 Śāntideva, *A Guide to the Bodhisattva's Way of Life* 4:32, 9a6.

95 Śāntideva, *A Guide to the Bodhisattva's Way of Life* 4:33, 9a7.

96 Śāntideva, *A Guide to the Bodhisattva's Way of Life* 4:30–31, 9a:5.

97 As the subsequent paragraph alludes, countering the afflictions
through conduct refers to refraining from their external expression in
body and speech. Countering them through meditation means meditation on the three scopes of the stages of the path (*lam rim*) teaching.
Countering them through view refers to seeing the emptiness of these
afflictions, their lack of any solid, real object of reference.

98 *A Guide to the Bodhisattva's Way of Life* 4:46d, 10a1.

99 It is difficult to determine what "the king Asaṅga" refers to. It is probably an allusion to a story from the scriptures.

100 Śāntideva, *A Guide to the Bodhisattva's Way of Life* 10:56, 40a:3.

101 Nāgārjuna, *Commentary on the Awakening Mind* 106, 42a:7. The
wording of these lines is slightly different in the Tengyur.

# Essential Mind Training

102 This sentence is somewhat obscure. Probably the author means that to take the defeat upon yourself means to avoid adding to your negative karma by retaliating in response to harm.

103 Śāntideva, *A Guide to the Bodhisattva's Way of Life* 6:111, 19a2.

104 *A Guide to the Bodhisattva's Way of Life* 6:2, 14b4.

105 This is the first of the three aspects of forbearance, the practices of which are explained in detail by Śāntideva in *A Guide to the Bodhisattva's Way of Life*. The remaining two are the forbearance of voluntarily accepting suffering and the forbearance that results from reflecting on the teachings.

106 This appears to be a slight variation of the first two lines of Nāgārjuna's *Precious Garland* 5:83. In Nāgārjuna's text, the lines read, "May their negativity ripen upon me, / and may my virtues ripen upon them."

107 Śāntideva, *A Guide to the Bodhisattva's Way of Life* 6:42, 16a5.

108 Śāntideva, *A Guide to the Bodhisattva's Way of Life* 6:47, 16b1.

109 Śāntideva, *A Guide to the Bodhisattva's Way of Life* 3:16, 7a5.

110 Source unidentified.

111 *Bde ba'i klu.* This text was not identified and the quote was not located in the Tengyur, though a text of the same title is attributed to Atiśa in another text.

112 "Definite goodness" (*nges legs*) refers to the attainments of nirvana and buddhahood.

113 Śāntideva, *A Guide to the Bodhisattva's Way of Life* 8:131, 28b4.

114 Śāntideva, *A Guide to the Bodhisattva's Way of Life* 9:152–53, 36b4.

115 Śāntideva, *A Guide to the Bodhisattva's Way of Life* 9:154ab, 36b6.

116 That is, we take the first two noble truths, suffering and its causes, of all sentient beings on to ourselves, and with respect to the two remaining noble truths—cessation and the path—we imagine giving away our potential realizations of these two to all beings.

117 Rahul Sankrityayan asserts that Serlingpa was "famous for his scholarship throughout the Buddhist world." See P. V. Bapat, ed., *2500 Years of Buddhism* (Delhi: Ministry of Information and Broadcasting, 1959), p. 202. The noted early twentieth-century Tibetan author and historian Gendün Chöphel opines that Serlingpa probably held the title of Dharma King (*dharmarāja*), a title often held by senior figures in the Southeast Asian Buddhist tradition.

118 The translation of this root text is based on the version found in Yeshé Döndrup's *Treasury of Gems* (pp. 41–42), which its author asserts is a critical edition based on consultation with the commentary found in

our present volume. He maintains that the version of this root text found in at least two editions of the *Great Collection*—a handwritten edition and a Mongolian blockprint edition—and also the version found in Sumpa Yeshé Paljor's (1704–88) collected works, all suffer from corruptions of spelling.

119 This list of four antidotes differs slightly in different texts. Some editions list the third as "a charm bringing closure to your miseries," which is probably incorrect, an error perpetuated by a corrupt spelling.

120 The act of sealing your practice with meditation on emptiness is a common Mahayana practice. For example, according to Mahayana teaching, the practice of each and every one of the six perfections must be completed with a meditation on the emptiness of what are known as the three factors—the object of the action, the agent, and the action itself. This ensures that your spiritual practice does not fall prey to the deeply ingrained tendency to grasp at things as possessing some kind of enduring reality, thus reinforcing your bondage to cyclic existence. The four acts of sealing referred to in this text, however—casting away, letting go, dismantling, and letting be—appear to be a unique approach.

121 It is difficult to assess the true authorship of this commentarial work. However, if the attribution to Serlingpa of its root text is valid, it is conceivable that Atiśa gave commentaries, or at least explanations, of the instructions contained in the root stanzas. Although the opening two paragraphs of this text are clearly not by Atiśa, as to the main body of the text, I will follow the traditional attribution of this commentary to Master Atiśa.

122 Source unidentified.

123 *True Union Tantra*, 158a3. These two lines are found also in the *Magical Net Tantra*, 131a3. They are also cited by Atiśa in his *Lamp for the Path to Enlightenment*, 240b2.

124 Candrakīrti, *Entering the Middle Way* 6:117, 210a1.

125 The four enlightened factors are the four enumerated in the first stanza of the root text.

126 See note 119 above.

127 For the three kinds of forbearance, see note 105 above.

128 On sealing spiritual practice with emptiness, see note 120 above.

129 This last sentence is effectively the colophon of this commentary on *Leveling Out All Conceptions*, and therefore the actual body of the text concludes here. The remaining part is composed of several citations

from sutras and tantras, all of which underline the point that great compassion is the core practice of a bodhisattva, whose sole aspiration is to bring about the welfare of other sentient beings. These citations may have been added later by a Tibetan editor, perhaps Könchok Gyaltsen himself.

130 *Heart of Amoghapāśa Sutra*, 281a1.

131 Buddhaśrījñāna, *Drop of Freedom*, 48b2.

132 Buddhaśrījñāna, *Drop of Freedom*, 48b5.

133 *Perfectly Gathering the Qualities [of Avalokiteśvara] Sutra*, 84a5.

134 A second text in *Mind Training: The Great Collection* entitled *Peacock's Neutralizing of Poison* is attributed to the same author and is similar in language and style.

135 In producing my translation of *Wheel of Sharp Weapons*, I had access to three different editions of the text. One is the version found in the original Tibetan volume of *Mind Training: The Great Collection*. The second was embedded in a lengthy commentary produced from the lecture notes taken from a teaching by the noted Geluk master Trichen Tenpa Rapgyé (1759–1815). The final version appeared in an anthology of Kadam teachings entitled *Treausury of Gems*, compiled by the nineteenth-century Mongolian author Yeshé Döndrup. Those interested in the philological comments on the variant readings between these different editions of the text may consult my notes in *Mind Training: The Great Collection*. Readers should also note that the numbering of the verses does not exist in the original and has been introduced for the convenience of translation. In organizing the lines of the poem into stanzas and introducing numbers for them, I have consulted primarily Trichen Tenpa Rapgyé's commentary and the topical outlines found in Losang Tamdrin's *Annotations*. In finalizing my translation, I benefited from the translation by Geshe Lhundub Sopa and Michael Sweet in *Peacock in the Poison Grove*, as well as the much earlier translation of the *Wheel of Sharp Weapons* published by the Library of Tibetan Works and Archives.

136 Literally, "enemy of Yama," the lord of death in the Buddhist pantheon. Yamāntaka is a wrathful meditation deity often said to be a manifestation of Mañjuśrī, the buddha of wisdom.

137 "Insights of learning and so on" refers to the three levels of understanding described in classical Buddhist texts: understanding derived from (1) learning, (2) critical reflection, and (3) meditation.

138 My reading of this line, substantially different from Sopa et al., is based

on Trichen's *Notes* (p. 36a). Trichen reads the line to demonstrate the contradiction between someone who aspires for material resources, which according to Buddhist teachings come about as a consequence of giving, yet indulges in such negative acts as stealing and extortion.

139 The Tibetan terms I have translated here as "divination" and "shamanism" are *mo* and *bon*. Although the term *bon* later became established as the name of Tibet's pre-Buddhist religion, the term can also simply refer to some form of village shamanism or animism. This idea of not relying on *mo* and *bon* appears to be an important theme in the early Kadam writings. For to do so is, according to the Kadam masters, to contradict the Buddhist practice of seeking refuge only in the Three Jewels.

140 The Tibetan *sa mtha'*, which literally means "remote areas," connotes areas that are outside the bounds of Dharma civilization. Hence my choice of the term "wilderness."

141 This is a sarcastic remark. In actual fact, clairvoyance can only arise from prolonged meditation practice.

142 Here "well-spoken words" (*legs bshad*) refers to the teachings of the Buddha and their subsequent commentarial treatises.

143 These two lines resonate very closely with two famous lines from the *Seven-Point Mind Training*.

144 "Existence and pacification" refers to the well-known Buddhist dichotomy of samsara (cyclic existence) and nirvana (its pacification).

145 The three wisdoms are the understandings mentioned above in note 137.

146 This last line suggests that the above song was sung as a self-exhortation by Maitrīyogi.

147 "Pure trainees" here refers to those bodhisattvas who have gained direct insight into emptiness, have attained the state of a noble one (*ārya*), and are, as a consequence, on one of the ten bodhisattva levels (*bhūmi*). "Purity" here connotes the bodhisattvas' transcendence of bondage to karma, for—following their direct realization of emptiness—they are no longer subject to the law of karma. According to the Mahayana scriptures, the Buddha's embodiment as enjoyment body is visible only to those sentient beings who are on the bodhisattva levels.

148 These are the first two lines of the Kashmiri master Śākyaśrībhadra's single-stanza root text. For a brief account of this Kashmiri master, especially his activity in Tibet, see Gö Lotsāwa's *Blue Annals*, vol. 2 (Sichuan: Minorities Press, 1984), pp. 1237–49; English translation

by George Roerich: *The Blue Annals* (Delhi: Motilal Banarsidass, 1988), pp. 1062–73.

149  "Impure trainees" here refers to all the spiritual aspirants who have not yet gained direct realization of emptiness and thus are not free from bondage to karma.

150  Gö Lotsāwa, *Blue Annals*, vol. 1, pp. 469–70; English translation: pp. 388–89.

151  This relates to a classic Mahayana formulation of three distinct types of compassion and loving-kindness, presented, for example, in the opening verses of Candrakīrti's *Entering the Middle Way*. The first, *focusing on sentient beings*, refers to the form of compassion that arises simply on the basis of taking suffering sentient beings as its focus. The second, *focusing on mere phenomena*, refers to a slightly more advanced form of compassion, where in addition to focusing on suffering, the person is also aware of the mere phenomenal natures of these suffering beings. Finally, *compassion with objectless focus* refers to an even more advanced level where the person is aware of the empty nature of the beings while being compassionate toward their suffering. This last form is totally free from any degree of objectification or clinging, thus is referred to as compassion of *objectless focus*, or nonreferential compassion.

152  Samantabhadra's expansive aspirations and vows, cited here, are probably drawn from the well-known work entitled *Vows of Good Conduct*, which is sometimes identified as the final section of the *Flower Ornament Scripture*. The recitation of this prayer, which has attracted commentaries from numerous Tibetan authors, is highly popular in Tibetan Buddhist communities, including the laity, and is often recited at funerals as well.

153  The obscurations of karma, of afflictions, and of subtle knowledge.

154  This echoes Śāntideva's *Guide to the Bodhisattva's Way of Life* 1:40.

155  For a detailed description of these factors, see the English translation of Tsongkhapa's *The Great Treatise*, vol. 2 (Ithaca, NY: Snow Lion Publications, 2002), pp. 76–80.

156  Śāntideva, *A Guide to the Bodhisattva's Way of Life* 1:9, 2a5.

157  A disciple of the Buddha renowned for the stability of his mindfulness and his effectiveness in spreading the teachings.

158  This is probably a typographical error and should be Neusurpa, who was a principal disciple of Gönpawa.

159  It is difficult to say when the well-known myth of the Mongol taming a tiger evolved in Tibet. It is a popular theme in Tibetan murals.

160 Shönu Gyalchok (*Compendium of Well-Uttered Insights*, p. 226) lists this second purpose as "the great successor to misery" (*sdug gi mjug mthud chen po*), consistent with *Leveling Out All Conceptions* (see page 132 above), which is probably one of the earliest sources of this concept. However, in his concluding sentence of this section below, Shönu Gyalchok refers to this as "the closure to misery," agreeing with the version here.

161 The original Tibetan for these two expressions, which I have translated as to "let go as best as I can" and to "let go so that it is wiped clean" is *gans legs la thong* and *byug legs la thong*. These expressions are somewhat opaque, so my translations are only suggestive.

162 "The three noble beings"—śrāvakas, pratyekabuddhas, and bodhisattvas—are called "noble" (*ārya*) because they have gained the direct realization of emptiness. The subtle obscuration to knowledge is the final barrier preventing their full enlightenment.

163 The wording of this line is slightly different in the *Root Lines*, where it reads, "When stability is attained, reveal the secret." Furthermore, as noted in my annotations to the *Root Lines*, it is not found in Chekawa's *Seven-Point Mind Training*.

164 The six directions are the four cardinal directions—east, south, west, and north—and above and below. This alludes to a well-known reductive analysis found in Vasubandhu's *Twenty Verses* (stanza 12) in which he critiques the concept of indivisible atoms. At the heart of the argument is the assertion that, even at the subtle-particle level, a material object will possess at least these six directional perspectives, which implies, at least conceptually, that the object in question remains divisible.

165 Saraha, *Songs of the Treasury of Dohas*, 73a4.

166 These two expressions—"continuum of compassion" and "its rationale"—appear to be vocabulary specific to this mind training instruction and are elaborated below.

167 I introduced these numbers to help the reader identify what the text later refers to as the five rationales for cultivating compassion toward those who harm you.

168 This appears to be a citation from Bhūripa's *Extensive Daily Confessions of Cakrasaṃvara* [*Practice*], 95a4.

169 This, too, appears to be a citation from Bhūripa's *Extensive Daily Confessions of Cakrasaṃvara* [*Practice*], 95a4. This and the line above appear in numerous works on mind training.

# Glossary

**accumulations** (*tshogs, sambhāra*). Sometimes translated also as *collections, accumulations* refer to the two principal classes of conditions to be cultivated for the attainment of buddhahood. The two are the accumulation of merit—which includes all the practices of compassion—and the accumulation of wisdom, the insight into emptiness.

**adverse conditions/adversities** (*rkyen ngan*). Refers to all types of conditions, circumstances, and events that are detrimental to well-being. These include ill health, tragic events, and harm from others. The mind training teachings focus on how to creatively turn these adversities into conditions favorable to spiritual practice.

**afflictions** (*nyon mongs, kleśa*). A class of dissonant mental states, including both thoughts and emotions, that have their root in ignorance. They are referred to as "afflictions" because they afflict the individual from deep within. The classical Abhidharma texts list six root afflictions—(1) attachment, (2) aversion, (3) conceit, (4) afflicted doubt, (5) ignorance, and (6) afflicted view—and twenty afflictions that are derivative of these root afflictions.

**Akaniṣṭha** (*'og min*). The highest realm of the form realms, where, according to Mahayana scriptures, the buddhas remain present in their enjoyment bodies.

**antidote** (*gnyen po*). Just as a specific medicine is seen as the antidote for a specific illness, in mind training practice, mental states such as compassion and loving-kindness are identified as antidotes against specific mental ills. Since one of the principal objectives of mind training practice is the purification of your mind, applying antidotes is an important recurrent theme in the mind training texts. The Tibetan term *gnyen po* is sometimes translated also as "remedy" or "counter factor" as well.

**aspiration** (*'dun pa, chanda*). In the context of mind training teaching, the term refers to a fundamental form of aspiration, such as your life's aspiration. One of the mind training precepts is to avoid misplaced aspiration, which means viewing the advantages of this life as admirable and aspiring for them.

**aspiration prayer** (*smon lam, praṇidhāna*). In the literary context, aspirational prayers in Tibetan are easily recognized by the presence of their ending particle *shog*, which is translated as "may such and such be." The Tibetan term *smon lam* is also sometimes translated simply as "prayer" or "prayer of aspiration."

**aspiring awakening mind** (*smon pa byang sems*). *See* awakening mind

**awakening mind** (*byang chub kyi sems, bodhicitta*). An altruistic intention to attain buddhahood for the benefit of all beings. The awakening mind is characterized by an *objective*, the full awakening of budhahood, and a *purpose*, the fulfillment of others' welfare.

Following the Indian Mahayana classics, the mind training texts speak of "training in the two awakening minds"—the *conventional awakening mind* and the *ultimate awakening mind*. The former refers to altruistic intention as defined above, while the latter refers to a direct realization of the emptiness of the fully awakened mind. In general usage, the term *awakening mind* is a synonym for the conventional awakening mind, which is in turn understood in terms of two levels. First is the *aspiring awakening mind*, which is likened to the intention of a person who wishes to travel somewhere; and the second is the *engaging awakening mind*, likened to the intention of the person who has actually embarked on the journey. This second level is realized when the aspirant commits him or herself, by means of a vow, to the actual fulfillment of the aim of bringing about others' welfare.

**basis-of-all** (*kun gzhi, ālaya*). There are two principal interpretations of what is meant by *basis-of-all* in the context of mind training. One interpretation is that it refers to an uncontrived mind (*sems ma bcos pa*), while the second interpretation maintains that it refers to the mind's emptiness. In its classical usage in Indian Buddhism, the term *ālaya* is assocated with the Yogācāra theory of mind, where *basis-of-all consciousness* (*kun gzhi rnam shes, ālayavijñāna*) refers to a foundational consciousness that is thought to be the repository of all our karmic imprints, propensities, and habitual tendencies.

**bodhisattva** (*byang chub sems dpa'*). A person who has cultivated the awakening mind and is on the path to buddhahood.

**clear light** (*'od gsal, prabhāsvara*). The term *clear light* is used in two senses in the present collection. It sometimes refers simply to the mind's ultimate empty nature, the emptiness of the stream of consciousness. In other contexts, it is used in a more Vajrayana sense as the subtlest and most constant aspect of the mind. The archetypal example is the "clear light of death" where all mental processes have ceased and only the subtlest, clear-light level of consciousness remains.

**clinging** (*zhen pa*). A mind or action that grasps to an object, quality, or a mental state.

**compassion** (*snying rje, karuṇā*). A mental state that wishes others to be free of suffering. *Compassion* is often used in mind training literature as a synonym for "great compassion" (*snying rje chen po*), a universal, nondiscriminatory compassion that wishes all beings to be free of suffering.

**conceptual elaboration** (*spros pa, prapañca*). A proliferation of thoughts that includes all forms of dichotomizing conceptualization, such as subject-object duality, as well as grasping at objects and their characteristics. The direct realization of emptiness is marked by total freedom from all such conceptual elaborations.

**conceptualization** (*rnam rtog, vicāra*). The Tibetan term *rnam rtog* has been translated as "conceptualization" and carries numerous connotations. (1) It can refer simply to thoughts, which unlike direct sensory experiences are mediated by language and concepts. (2) However, it can also refer specifically to dichotomizing thoughts that lead to the objectification and reification of things and events. (3) Sometimes, the term may be used in the negative sense of "false conceptualization." In the context of this volume, *rnam rtog* carries more the second and third meaning.

**confession/purification** (*bshags pa, deśanā*). The practice for cleansing your past negative karma. A successful practice of purification must involve the application of antidotes endowed with four powers: (1) the power of eradication (by means of repentance), (2) the power of applying antidotes, (3) the power of turning away from the errors, and (4) the power of the basis (refuge in the Three Jewels).

**conventional awakening mind** (*kun rdzob byang chub sems*). *See* awakening mind

**conventional truth** (*kun rdzob bden pa, saṃvṛtisatya*). *See* two truths

**cyclic existence** (*'khor ba, saṃsāra*). The perpetual cycle of birth, death, and rebirth within an existence conditioned by karma and afflictions. Freedom from cyclic existence is characterized as *nirvana*, the "transcendence of sorrow."

**defilement** (*sgrib pa, āvaraṇa*). Literally "obscuration," *defilement* refers to the factors (such as mental and emotional states as well as their imprints, propensities, and habitual tendencies) that obstruct us from attaining liberation or the full omniscience of buddhahood. There are two main categories of defilements. The first, "defilements in the form of the afflictions and their seeds," obstructs the attainment of liberation. And the second, "defilements in the form of subtle propensities of these mental states and the deep habitual tendencies for dualistic perceptions," obstructs the attainment of buddhahood.

**dharmakāya** (*chos sku*). One of the three bodies of buddhahood. *Dharmakāya*, which literally means "truth body," refers to the ultimate reality of a buddha's enlightened mind—unborn, free from the limits of conceptual elaboration, empty of intrinsic existence, naturally radiant, beyond duality, and spacious like the sky. The other two buddha bodies, the buddha body of enjoyment (*saṃbhogakāya*) and the buddha body of emanation (*nirmāṇakāya*), are progressively grosser bodies that arise naturally from the basic dharmakāya state.

**emptiness** (*stong pa nyid, śūnyatā*). According to the Perfection of Wisdom scriptures of Mahayana Buddhism, all things and events, including our own existence, are devoid of any independent, substantial, and intrinsic reality. This emptiness of independent existence is phenomena's ultimate mode of being—the way they actually are. The theory of emptiness is most systematically developed in the writings of the second-century Indian thinker Nāgārjuna, who demonstrated the emptiness of all things and events, both external and internal, through logical reasoning. Since our deeply ingrained tendency is to perceive and grasp a substantial reality in all phenomena, we engender a cycle of conceptualization, objectification, grasping, and bondage. Only through bringing an end to this cycle, Nāgārjuna argues, can we begin the path to liberation.

**five aggregates** (*phung po lnga, pañca skandha*). The five key physical and mental elements that, according to Buddhist psychology, constitute the basis of the identity of a person. The five are form, feeling, discrimination, mental formations, and consciousness, each of which is referred to as an aggregate to underscore their composite nature.

**five heinous acts** (*mtshams med lnga*). Literally meaning "without a break," these deeds are of such heinous nature that the perpetrator will depart to the lowest forms of existence with no break at all after death. The five are killing one's father, killing one's mother, killing an arhat, wounding the body of a buddha, and creating a schism within the monastic community.

**five poisons** (*dug lnga*). The afflictions of attachment, anger, delusion, pride, and jealousy, which are often characterized as "poisons" of the mind. This is a slightly more extended list of the *three poisons*—attachment, anger, and delusion.

**freeing the remedy too in its own place** (*gnyen po nyid kyang rang sar grol ba*). This means that, in applying antidotes against the afflictions, you need to avoid grasping at the antidotes themselves. This instruction echoes the Mahayana exhortation to remember that emptiness, too, is empty of intrinsic existence.

**hero** (*dpa' bo, vīra*). In some of the verse texts featured in this volume, the term *hero* is sometimes used as an epithet for a bodhisattva, to connote the courage to willingly plunge into the world of suffering and take it upon oneself.

**loving-kindness** (*byams pa, maitrī*). As a "mental factor wishing others to achieve happiness," *loving-kindness* is said to be the other facet of compassion. The mind training texts give specific instructions on cultivating loving-kindness. This loving-kindness is to be distinguished from the loving-kindness of cherishing others as dear, which is step 4 in the seven-point cause-and-effect method of cultivating the awakening mind.

**Māra's activity** (*bdud las*). In Mahayana thought, often a detrimental thought or action is described as "Māra's activity," implying that it is the product of the beguiling forces of the afflictions. The concept of Māra goes back to the earliest Buddhist literature, where it is a personification of the basic obstructive forces—internal afflictions, such as anger, desire, and delusion. In fact, one of the "twelve deeds of the Buddha" is his gaining victory over the forces of Māra. Classical Buddhist texts list four such *māras*: (1) the māra of afflictions, (2) the māra of death, (3) the māra of conditioned aggregates, and (4) the māra of beguiling desire (literally, the "son of devas").

**meditation** (*sgom, bhāvanā*). Both the Sanskrit and the Tibetan terms for meditation connote the notion of cultivation, such as the cultivation of certain mental habit. The Tibetan term in particular carries a strong sense of cultivating familiarity, be it with a chosen object, topic, or a particular way of thinking or being. Principally, there are two kinds of meditation: absorptive meditation (*'jog sgom*), which is characterized by single-pointed focus; and analytic meditation (*dpyad sgom*), which is characterized primarily by deep analysis. There are other types of meditation, too, such as visualization, aspiration, or cultivation. Given this diversity, different words—"contemplate," "meditate," "visualize," and "cultivate"—have been used to translate the Tibetan verb *sgom pa*, depending upon the context.

**meditative absorption** (*ting nge 'dzin, samādhi*). Meditative absorption is the state where the mind is totally focused in single-pointed absorption on a chosen object. The Sanskrit term *samādhi* and its Tibetan equivalent have several different meanings in different contexts. In the context of the Abhidharma taxonomy of mental factors, the term refers to a mental factor whose primary function is to ensure the stability of the mind. This mental factor is part of a group of mental factors present in all unmistaken cognitions. *Meditative absorption* can also refer to a specific advanced meditative state, such as the direct single-pointed realization of emptiness. Finally, the term can refer to a specific meditation practice, such as meditative absorption on compassion.

**meditative equipoise** (*mnyam gzhag, samāhita*). A session of single-pointed fusion with the chosen object of meditation. Sometimes *meditative equipoise* is simply a synonym for "meditation session" in contrast to the practices pursued between sessions. In the *Seven-Point Mind Training*, for example, the practices of cultivating the two awakening minds are regarded as practices for the actual meditation session, while all other practices are described as those of the intervening periods.

**method** (*thabs, upāya*). *Method* refers to the altruistic deeds of the bodhisattva, including the cultivation of compassion and the awakening mind. In Mahayana Buddhism, the union of method and wisdom is central to understanding the path.

**negative action** (*sdig pa/sdig pa'i las, pāpa/pāpakarma*). Actions of body, speech, and mind that are actually harmful or potentially harmful. Negative actions are motivated by any of the three poisons of the mind—attachment, aversion, and delusion. Though used interchangeably in the texts with *mi dge ba* or *mi dge ba'i las* (Tibetan equivalents for the Sanskrit terms *akuśala* or *akuśa-lakarma*) and translated as "nonvirtuous action," the Tibetan term *sdig pa* and its Sanskrit equivalent actually carry a heavier, sin-like connotation. Hence I have chosen to distinguish their usage by choosing two different English renderings: "negative" and "nonvirtuous." The classical Buddhist texts list ten classes of negative actions: three actions of body, which are (1) killing, (2) stealing, and (3) sexual misconduct; four actions of speech, which are (4) lying, (5) engaging in divisive speech, (6) using harsh words, and (7) indulging in frivolous speech; and three actions of mind, which are (8) covetousness, (9) ill will, and (10) wrong views. *See also* nonvirtuous karma

**noble one** (*'phags pa, ārya*). A being on the path who has gained direct realization of the truth. Noble ones are contrasted with ordinary beings (*so so'i ske bo, pṛthagjana*), whose understanding of the truth remains bound by language and concepts.

**nonvirtuous karma** (*mi dge ba/mi dge ba'i las, akuśala/akuśala-karma*). Although in most Buddhist texts the term *akauśalakarma* (nonvirtuous action) is used interchangeably with *pāpakarma* (negative action), etymologically the Sanskrit term *akuśala* connotes an act that is unskillful rather than negative. Similarly, the Tibetan equivalent of the term *mi dge ba* connotes an act that is not auspicious or virtuous. *See also* negative action

**obscuration to knowledge, subtle.** *See* defilement

**penetrative insight** (*lhag mthong, vipaśyanā*). An advanced meditative state where the meditator has successfully attained physical and mental pliancy because of having applied analytic meditation on a basis of tranquil abiding. Sometimes the term is also used generically to embrace all analytic, as opposed to absorptive, meditation practices.

**perfection of wisdom** (*sher phyin, prajñāpāramitā*). One of the six perfections that lie at the heart of the practice of the bodhisattva. Classical Mahayana texts apply the term in three principal ways. In the context of the resultant stage, the term refers the perfected wisdom of a fully awakened buddha, who is free of all defilements and directly perceives the two truths—conventional and ultimate—of all phenomena spontaneously in a single mental act. In terms of the path, *perfection of wisdom* refers to the bodhisattva's direct realization of emptiness, a wisdom that is in perfect union with the method side of the path. Finally, this term also refers to a specific subdivision of the Mahayana scriptures that outline the essential aspects of these paths and their resultant state. The *Perfection of Wisdom in Eight Thousand Lines*, the *Heart Sūtra*, and the *Diamond Cutter* are some of the most well-known Perfection of Wisdom scriptures.

**pith instructions** (*man ngag, upadeśa*). Sometimes translated simply as "instruction," *pith instruction* connotes a specialized kind of advice. This Tibetan word and the term *gdams ngag*, which has been translated as "advice," are both equivalents of a single Sanskrit term *upadeśa*. *Man ngag* connotes an instruction suited only to select practitioners. Often, *man ngag* also refers to an oral lineage.

**pristine cognition** (*ye shes, jñāna*). Often contrasted with ordinary consciousness (*rnam shes*), *pristine cognition* (*ye shes*) refers to a buddha's fully awakened wisdom and also to the uncontaminated gnosis of the noble ones that is characterized by the direct realization of emptiness. Some translate the Sanskrit term and its Tibetan equivalent as "wisdom" or "gnosis."

**pratyekabuddhas** (*rang sangs rgyas*). These "self-realized ones" aspire for their own liberation from cyclic existence and, unlike śrāvakas, seek liberation primarily on the basis of their own autonomous understanding rather than relying on instruction from others. In addition, they are said to accumulate both merit and wisdom for a much longer period than śrāvakas. The distinction between the śrāvaka and the pratyekabuddha varies among different philosophical schools.

**remedy** (*gnyen po*). *See* antidote

**self-cherishing** (*rang gces 'dzin*). The deeply ingrained thought that cherishes the welfare of your own self above all others and makes you oblivious to others' well-being. This is one of the "twin demons" (*gong po gnyis*) that lie within our hearts and serve as the source of all misfortune and downfall (the other twin demon being grasping at selfhood). These two thoughts—self-cherishing and self-grasping—are the primary focus of combat in the mind training practice.

**self-grasping** (*bdag 'dzin, ātmagṛha*). Instinctively believing in the intrinsic existence of your own self as well of the external world. *Self* here means a substantial, truly existing identity. The wisdom that realizes emptiness eliminates this self-grasping. *See also* self-cherishing

**śrāvakas** (*nyan thos*). Disciples of the Buddha whose primary spiritual objective is to attain liberation from the cycle of existence. The Sanskrit term and its Tibetan equivalent are sometimes translated as "hearers" (which stays close to the literal meaning) or as "pious attendants." Śrāvakas are often paired with pratyekabuddhas, who seek liberation on the basis of autonomous practice as opposed to listening to others' instructions.

**stages of the path** (*lam rim*). A genre of instruction on the Mahayana Buddhist path that evolved from Atiśa's *Lamp for the Path to Enlightenment*. This short text lays out the essence of the entire teachings of the Buddha within a graduated framework of practices that are geared to three levels of mental capacity. Tsongkhapa's *Great Exposition of the Stages of the Path* is the most well known of the later Tibetan works inspired by Atiśa's text.

**substantial existence** (*bden par yod pa/bden par grub pa*). A belief that things and events, including your own self, possess a true existence definable in terms of their elementary constituents (atom-like particles) or in terms of characteristics like causes, conditions, and effects.

**substantial reality** (*bden pa'i dngos po*). A belief that things and events possess substantial existence.

**suchness** (*de bzhin nyid, tattva/tathatā*). The reality of things as they are; often used as a synonym for *emptiness*.

**sugata**. Literally, "one gone to bliss"; a buddha.

**supplication** (*gsol 'debs*). An appeal or request written often in verse and directed to an object of veneration, such as the Three Jewels or your spiritual teacher.

**tathāgata** (*de bzhin gshegs pa, tathāgata*). Literally, "thus-gone one"; an epithet for a buddha.

**Tengyur** (*bstan 'gyur*). The section of the Tibetan Buddhist canon that contains primarily works of classical Indian masters translated from Sanskrit.

**Three Jewels** (*dkon mchog gsum, triratna*). The Buddha Jewel, the Dharma Jewel, and the Sangha Jewel together constitute the true object of refuge in Buddhism. You take refuge in the Buddha as the true teacher, in the Dharma as the true teaching, and in the Sangha (the spiritual community) as the true companions on the path.

**torma** (*gtor ma*). A cake for ritual offerings made from dough. Often cone-shaped and composed of yak butter and barley flour, *torma* can be as simple as a dough ball or elaborately crafted with colorful butter ornamentation.

**tranquil abiding** (*zhi gnas, śamatha*). An advanced meditative state where the meditator has attained a physical and mental pliancy derived from focusing the mind. It is characterized by stable single-pointed attention on a chosen object with all mental distractions calmed. Tranquil abiding is an essential basis for cultivating *penetrative insight*.

**two truths** (*bden pa gnyis, satyadvaya*). The concept of two levels of reality, *two truths*, is employed in all schools of Buddhism to explain their understanding of the nature of reality. What constitutes the conventional truth and what constitutes the ultimate truth differs among these schools. According to the Middle Way school, the perspective adopted in most of the mind training texts, *ultimate truth* refers to emptiness—the absence of the intrinsic existence of all phenomena. In contrast, *conventional truth* refers to the empirical aspect of reality as experienced through perception, thought, and language.

**ultimate awakening mind** (*don dam byang chub sems*). *See* awakening mind

**ultimate expanse** (*chos dbyings, dharmadhātu*). Often used as a synonym for *emptiness* and *suchness*, the term refers to the ultimate underlying truth of all things—namely their empty nature. This ultimate underlying truth constitutes the expanse from which arises the entire world of diversity, cause and effect, identity and difference, and so on, that characterizes our everyday world of existence.

**ultimate nature** (*gnas lugs*). Refers to the ultimate mode of being of things, which is *emptiness*. Hence the expression, "emptiness, the ultimate nature of phenomena" (*chos rnams kyi gnas lugs stong pa nyid*).

**ultimate truth** (*don dam bden pa, paramārthasatya*). *See* two truths

**virtuous karma** (*dge ba / dge ba'i las, kuśala/kuśalakarma*). Actions of body, speech, and mind motivated by wholesome states of mind, such as nonattachment, nonaversion, and nondelusion; these are actions either actually or potentially beneficial for others and one's own self. *See also* nonvirtuous karma

**wisdom** (*shes rab, prajñā*). The Sanskrit term *prajñā* and its Tibetan equivalent *shes rab* have different applications depending upon the context. In the Abhidharma taxonomy of mental factors, *prajñā* refers to a specific mental factor that helps evaluate the various properties or qualities of an object. The term can refer simply to intelligence or mental aptitude. In the context of the Mahayana path, *prajñā* refers to the wisdom aspect of the path constituted primarily by deep insight into the emptiness of all phenomena. Hence the term *prajñā* and its Tibetan equivalent are translated variously as "wisdom," "insight," or "intelligence."

**yoga** (*rnal 'byor*). Literally meaning "union," *yoga* refers to advanced meditative practices, especially in the context of Buddhist tantra. The Tibetan term *rnal 'byor* has the added connotation of "uniting one's mind with the nature of reality."

# Bibliography

## SCRIPTURES

*Ākāśagarbha Sutra. Ākāśagarbhasūtra. Nam mkha'i snying po'i mdo.*
Toh 260, mdo sde, *za.* P926, *zhu.*

*Condensed Perfection of Wisdom in Stanzas. Prajñāpāramitāsaṃ-*
*cayagāthā. Shes rab kyi pha rol tu phyin pa bsdud pa tshigs su bcad*
*pa.* Toh 13, shes phyin, *ka.* P735, *tsi.*

*Flower Ornament Scripture. Avataṃsakasūtra. Sangs rgyas phal po*
*che zhes bya ba shin tu rab tu rgyas pa.* Toh 44, phal chen, *ka–a.*
P761, *yi–hi.*

*Heart of Amoghapāśa Sutra.* (Referred to also as the *Amoghapāśa*
*Tantra.) Amoghapāśahṛdayasūtra. 'Phags pa don yod zhags pa'i*
*snying po.* Toh 682, rgyud, *ba.* P366, *ma.*

*Magical Net Tantra. Māyājālatantra. Rgyud kyi rgyal po chen po sgyu*
*'phrul dra ba.* Toh 466, rgyud 'bum, *ja.* P102, *ja.*

*Perfectly Gathering the Qualities [of Avalokiteśvara] Sutra. Dharma -*
*saṃgītisūtra. Chos yang dag par sdud pa'i mdo.* Toh 238, mdo sde,
*zha.* P904, *vu.*

*Teachings of Vimalakīrti Sutra. Vimalakīrtinirdeśasūtra. Dri ma med*
*par grags pas bstan pa.* Toh 176, mdo sde, *ma.* P843, *bu.*

*True Union Tantra. Sampuṭatantra. Yang dag par sbyor ba'i rgyud.*
Toh 381, rgyud, *ga.* P26, *ga.*

*Vajra Peak Tantra. Vajraśekharatantra. Gsang ba rnal 'byor chen po'i*
*rgyud rdo rje rtse mo.* Toh 480, rgyud, *nya.* P113.

*Vows of Good Conduct. Bhadracaryāpraṇidhāna. Bzang po spyod pa'i*
*smon lam.* Toh 1095, gzungs bsdus, *vam.* P716, *ya.* This is found
also as part 4 of the *Flower Ornament Scripture.*

*Essential Mind Training*

## Authored Works

Āryaśūra. *Garland of Birth Stories. Jātakamālā. Skyes rabs kyi rgyud.*
  Toh 4150, skyes rabs, *hu.* P5650, *ki.*

Asaṅga. *Levels of the Bodhisattva. Bodhisattvabhūmi. Byang chub
  sems dpa'i sa.* Toh 4037, sems tsam, *vi.* P5538, *zhi.* For an English
  translation of the chapter on ethics, see Mark Tatz (1986). The
  chapter on reality has been translated by Janice Willis in *On
  Knowing Reality: The Tattvārtha Chapter of Asaṅga's Bodhisattvabhūmi* (New York: Columbia University Press, 1979).

Atiśa Dīpaṃkara. *Garland of Unblemished Precious Gems. Vim-
  alaratnalekha. Dri ma med pa rin po che'i spring yig.* Toh 4188,
  spring yig, *nge.* P5688, *nge.*

———. *Lamp for the Path to Enlightenment. Bodhipathapradīpa.
  Byang chub lam gyi sgron ma.* Toh 3947, dbu ma, *khi.* P5343, *ki.*
  For an English translation, see Geshe Sonam Rinchen's *Atisha's
  Lamp for the Path to Enlightenment.* Ruth Sonam, trans. Ithaca,
  NY: Snow Lion Publications, 1997.

Bapat, P. V., ed. *2500 Years of Buddhism.* Delhi: Ministry of Information and Broadcasting, Government of India, 1959; reprint 1987.

Bhūripa. *Extensive Daily Confessions of Cakrasaṃvara [Practice].
  Dpal 'khor lo mde mchog gi rgyun bshags rgyas pa.* Toh 1533,
  rgyud 'grel, *za.* P2244, *pha.*

Buddhaśrījñāna. *Drop of Freedom. Muktitilaka. Grol ba'i thig le.* Toh
  1859, rgyud 'grel, *di.* P2722, *ti.*

Candrakīrti. *Entering the Middle Way. Madhyamakāvatāra. Dbu
  ma la 'jug pa'i tshig le'ur byas pa.* Toh 3861, dbu ma, *'a.* P5262, *'a.*
  An English translation of this work from the Tibetan can be
  found in C. W. Huntington, Jr. (1989).

Chegom Sherap Dorjé (ca. twelfth century), compiler. *Miscellaneous Sayings of the Kadam Masters. Bka' gdams gsung bgros thor
  bu.* English translation in Thupten Jinpa, trans., *The Book of
  Kadam* (2008).

Chim Namkha Drak (1210–85). *Biography of Master Atiśa. Jo bo rje'i
  rnam thar rgyas pa yongs grags.* In *The Book of Kadam (Bka'*

270

*gdams glegs bam*), vol. 1, pp. 44–228. Typeset edition, Kansu: Nationalities Press, 1993.

Dalai Lama, His Holiness the. *The Compassionate Life.* Boston: Wisdom Publications, 2001.

——. *Lighting the Way.* Ithaca, NY: Snow Lion Publications, 2004.

——. *Open Heart.* New York: Little, Brown, 2002.

——. *Transforming the Mind.* Translated by Thupten Jinpa. London: Thorsons, 2000.

Dharmakīrti. *Thorough Exposition of Valid Cognition. Pramāṇavārttika. Tshad ma rnam 'grel gyi tshigs le'ur byas pa.* Toh 4210, tshad ma, *ce.* P5709, *ce.*

Dromtönpa (1005–65). *Source of Teachings. Chos kyi 'byung gnas.* In *The Book of Kadam,* vol. 1, pp. 229–90. Typeset edition, Kansu: Nationalities Press, 1993.

Dunne, John, and Sarah McClintock, trans. *The Precious Garland.* Boston: Wisdom Publications, 1997.

Eimer, Helmut. "The Development of the Biographical Tradition Concerning Atiśa (Dīpaṃkaraśrījñāna)." *The Journal of the Tibet Society, London* 2 (1982): 41–51.

Gö Lotsawa Shönu Pal (1392–1481). *The Blue Annals. Deb ther sngon po.* Typeset edition in two volumes, Sichuan: Minorities Press, 1984. English translation by George N. Roerich as *The Blue Annals.* Delhi: Motilal Banarsidass; reprint 1988.

Hopkins, Jeffrey, trans. *Buddhist Advice for Living and Liberation: Nāgārjuna's Precious Garland.* Ithaca, NY: Snow Lion Publications, 1998.

Hortön Namkha Pal (1373–1447). *Mind Training: Rays of Sun. Blo sbyong nyi ma'i 'od zer.* Xylograph edition reprinted by Tibetan Cultural Printing Press, Dharamsala, 1986. English translation by Brian Beresford of this text is available under the title *Mind Training Like the Rays of Sun.* Ed. by Jeremy Russell. Dharamsala: Library of Tibetan Works and Archives, 1992.

Huntington, C. W., Jr., and Geshe Namgyal Wangchen. *The Emptiness of Emptiness.* Honolulu: University of Hawaii, 1989.

Jamgön Kongtrül (1831–90), ed. *Treasury of Instructions. Gdams ngag mdzod.* Xylograph edition. Delhi: Lungtok and Gyaltsen; reprint 1971.

Jinpa, Thupten, trans. *The Book of Kadam: The Core Texts.* The Library of Tibetan Classics 2. Boston: Wisdom Publications, 2008.

———. *Mind Training: The Great Collection.* Compiled by Shönu Gyalchok and Könchok Gyaltsen. The Library of Tibetan Classics 1. Boston: Wisdom Publications, 2006.

Karmapa Rangjung Dorjé (1284–1339). *One Hundred Birth Stories. Skyes rabs brgya pa.* Typeset edition in *Gangs can rigs brgya'i sgo 'byed lde mig,* vol. 22. Beijing: Nationalities Press, 1995.

Lindtner, Christian. *Nāgārjuniana: Studies in the Writings and Philosophy of Nāgārjuna.* Delhi: Motilal Banarsidass, 1982; reprint 1990.

Losang Tamdrin (1867–1937). *Annotations on the Wheel of Sharp Weapons Mind Training. Blo sbyong mtshon cha 'khor lo'i mchan. The Collected Works of Rje btsun Blo bzang rta mgrin,* vol. *ka.* Delhi: Guru Deva Lama, 1975.

Maitreya. *Ornament of Mahayana Sutras. Mahāyānasūtrālaṃkāra. Theg pa chen po mdo sde'i rgyan.* Toh 4020, sems tsam, *phi.* P5521, *phi.*

Nāgārjuna. *Commentary on the Awakening Mind. Bodhicittavivaraṇa. Byang chub sems kyi 'grel pa.* Toh 1800, rgyud 'grel, *ngi.* P2665, *gi.* An English translation is in Lindtner (1982).

———. *Friendly Letter. Suhṛllekha. Bshes pa'i spring yig.* Toh 4182, spring yig, *nge.* P5682, *nge.* English translation in Tharchin and Engle (1979).

———. *Precious Garland. Ratnāvalī. Rgyal po la gtam bya ba rin po che'i phreng ba.* Toh 4158, skyes rabs, *ge.* P5658, *nge.* English translations in Hopkins (1998) and in Dunne and McClintock (1997).

Phabongkha Dechen Nyingpo (1978–1941). *Root Text of the Seven-Point Mind Training. Blo sbyong don bdun ma'i rtsa tshig. The Collected Works,* vol. *ka.* English translation by Michael Richards in Pabongka Rinpoche, *Liberation in the Palm of Your Hand,* pp. 726–30. Rev. ed. Boston: Wisdom Publications, 2006.

Sangyé Gompa (1179–1250). *Public Explication of Mind Training. Blo sbyong tshogs bshad ma.* Entry 34 of *Mind Training: The Great Collection*, pp. 313–417.

Śāntideva. *Compendium of Trainings. Śikṣāsamuccaya. Bslab pa kun las btus pa.* Ṭoh 3939 and 3940, dbu ma, *khi.* P5336, *ki.* English translation from Sanskrit by Cecil Bendall and W. H. D. Rouse under the title *Śikṣā Samuccaya: A Compendium of Buddhist Doctrine.* Delhi: Motilal Banarsidass; reprint 1971.

———. *A Guide to the Bodhisattva's Way of Life. Bodhicaryāvatāra. Byang chub sems dpa'i spyod pa la 'jug pa.* Toh 3871, dbu ma, *la.* P5272, *la.* Several English translations of this work exist, including Stephen Batchelor's *Guide to the Bodhisattva's Way of Life* (Dharamsala: Library of Tibetan Works and Archives, 1979), the Padmakara Translation Group's *The Way of the Bodhisattva* (Boston: Shambhala Publications, 1997), Alan and Vesna Wallace's *A Guide to the Bodhisattva Way of Life* (Ithaca, NY: Snow Lion Publications, 1997), and Kate Crosby and Andrew Skilton's *Bodhicaryāvatāra* (New York: Oxford University Press, 1995).

Saraha. *Songs of the Treasury of Dohas. Dohākoṣagīti. Do ha mdzod kyi klu.* Toh 2224, rgyud 'grel, *vi.* P3068, *mi.* English translation in Herbert Guenther, *The Royal Song of Saraha.* Seattle: University of Washington, 1969.

Shönu Gyalchok (fourteenth century). *Mind Training: Compendium of Well-Uttered Insights. Blo sbyong legs bshad kun btus.* Xylograph, Dergé edition. Delhi: Ngawang Topgyal; reprint 1996.

Sopa, Geshe Lhundub, with Michael Sweet and Leonard Zwilling. *Peacock in the Poison Grove: Two Buddhist Texts on Training the Mind.* Boston: Wisdom Publications, 2001.

Tatz, Mark. *Asanga's Chapter on Ethics with the Commentary of Tsong-kha-pa.* Berkeley: University of California, 1986.

Tharchin, Geshe Lobsang, and Artemus Engle. *Nāgārjuna's Letter to a Friend with a Commentary by Venerable Rendawa Zhon-nu Lo-dro.* Dharamsala: Library of Tibetan Works and Archives, 1979.

Thokmé Sangpo (1295–1369). *Commentary on the Seven-Point Mind Training.* The full text in volume 3 of Jamgön Kongtrül's *Treasury of Instructions.* Delhi: Lungtok and Gyaltsen; reprint 1971.

Trichen Tenpa Rapgyé (1759–1815). *Ambrosia Giving Birth to Shoots of Altruistic Deeds: Notes on the Wheel of Sharp Weapons. Blo sbyong mtshon cha 'khor lo'i zin bris gzhan phan myu gu bskyed pa'i bdud rtsi. The Collected Works of Thri chen Bstan pa rab rgyas,* vol. 3. Dharamsala: Library of Tibetan Works and Archives, 1985.

Tsongkhapa (1357–1419). *The Great Treatise on the Stages of the Path to Enlightenment. Byang chub lam rim chen mo. The Collected Works of Tsongkhapa,* vol. *pha.* Xylograph edition reprinted by Guru Deva Lama in Delhi, 1978. Typeset edition, Kansu: Minorities Press, 1985. English translation of this work is available as *The Great Treatise on the Stages of the Path to Enlightenment,* vols. 1–3. The Lamrim Chenmo Translation Committee; Guy Newland, ed.; Joshua W. C. Cutler, editor-in-chief. Ithaca, NY: Snow Lion Publications, 2000, 2002, and 2004.

Vasubandhu. *Twenty Verses. Viṃśatikā. Nyi shu pa' tshig le'ur byas pa.* Toh 4056, sems tsam, *shi.* P5557, *si.* English translation in Stefan Anacker, *Seven Works of Vasubandhu, The Buddhist Psychological Doctor.* Delhi: Motilal Banarsidass, 1984.

Yeshé Döndrup (1792–1855). *Treasury of Gems: Selected Anthology of the Well-Uttered Insights of the Teachings of the Precious Kadam Tradition. Legs par bshad pa bka' gdams rin po che'i gsung gi gces btus legs bshad nor bu'i bang mdzod.* Typeset edition, Kansu: Nationalities Press, 1995.

# Index of Names and Titles

## Index of Names and Titles

# About Thupten Jinpa

THUPTEN JINPA was trained as a monk at the Shartse College of Ganden monastic university where he achieved the highest rank of Geshe Lharampa, and he holds a Ph.D. in religious studies from Cambridge University. He has been the principal English-language translator for His Holiness the Dalai Lama for more than two decades and has translated and edited numerous bestselling books by the Dalai Lama. Jinpa's own works include *Self, Reality and Reason in Tibetan Philosophy* and several volumes in *The Library of Tibetan Classics*. An adjuct professor at McGill University and a scholar at the Center for Compassion and Altruism Research and Education (CCARE) at Stanford University, Jinpa is currently the president of the Institute of Tibetan Classics in Montreal, where he lives with his wife and two daughters.

# About Wisdom Publications

WISDOM PUBLICATIONS is dedicated to offering works relating to and inspired by Buddhist traditions.

To learn more about us or to explore our other books, please visit our website at www.wisdompubs.org.

You can subscribe to our e-newsletter or request our print catalog online, or by writing to:

Wisdom Publications
199 Elm Street
Somerville, Massachusetts 02144 USA

You can also contact us at 617-776-7416, or email us at info@wisdompubs.org.

Wisdom is a nonprofit, charitable 501(c)(3) organization and donations in support of our mission are tax deductible.

Wisdom Publications is affiliated with the Foundation for the Preservation of the Mahayana Tradition (FPMT).